WHAT HAPPENS IN THE FAMILY

A STORY OF SURVIVAL

A.M. YOUNG

Copyright © 2020 by A.M. Young

ISBN: 978-0-578-76250-0

All rights reserved.

No part of this book may be reproduced in any form or by any electronic or mechanical means, including information storage and retrieval systems, without written permission from the author, except for the use of brief quotations in a book review.

CONTENTS

1. Ties That Bind	1
2. The Morning After	7
3. Sunday School	10
4. Sins of the Father	13
5. Near Death	17
6. Brotherly Love	21
7. Love Thy Neighbor	24
8. It Takes a Village	29
9. Broken Vows	35
10. Family Traditions	41
11. Evicted	46
12. Abandoned	49
13. Teachers	53
14. School Days	56
15. Bonding	60
16. A Preying Family	63
17. Betrayed	67
18. Thanksgiving Dinner	71
19. Coming of Age	74
20. Stalked	77
21. New Beginnings	81
22. Statutory	84
23. Mistakes	91
24. A Teenage Love	95
25. Growing Up	100
26. Fathers and Daughters	104
27. Relations	110
28. Brothers	112
29. Shattered	115
30. Healing	119
31. A Dream Deferred	121

32. Revelations	125
33. Goodbyes	127
34. Spiral	130
35. Lessons in Love	138
36. Snapped	142
Epilogue	149
About the Author	153

WHAT HAPPENS IN THE FAMILY

CHAPTER 1
TIES THAT BIND

Three-year-old Ava Jackson was bouncing up and down in the front seat of the car. She could not seem to keep still. Her mom, Jenney had long since given up telling her to sit down. Ava's energy seemed to know no bounds. She was staring out the window and pointing at everything they passed. She jumped up and down a little harder when she could see the little green store. Jenney sometimes stopped there and bought her chocolate milk. This time, she drove right past.

Ava loved to look at the horses, but only from the moving car. She thought they looked like magical beings, but she did not like to get too close. Her father Carl had stopped at the large farm once to let Ava have a better look. As they walked closer to the fence, Ava had reached for her father's hand. She thought the horses looked big and scary when she was outside staring up at them. She preferred to watch them from the car.

The car once belonged to Ava's late grandma, Verna. She had died just a few months before, in February, right after Ava turned three. Ava used to like visiting Grandma Verna at her house. She always gave Ava homemade cake and took her outside to play. She would give Ava big hugs and kisses and tell her stories from the Bible. She would let Ava watch tv with her. They never missed an episode of the Price is Right because that was their favorite show.

Ava was sad when they found her. She was riding in Grandma's Chrysler with her mom that day too. The sun had gone down, and the day was just starting to fade into darkness. The faintest traces of daylight were visible through the trees. They pulled up into the yard at the back of the house and got out of the car. She had walked with her mom to the back door. As they approached, Ava grabbed for her mother's hand. Her pulse began to race. The place was much too quiet. The crickets seemed to have stopped their chirping and even the frogs went silent. Something did not feel right. As they pushed the door open, Ava saw Grandma's body on the floor. Stunned by the sight, Ava just stared. She could feel her heart slamming painfully in her chest as she gazed down. Grandma's left arm had fallen to the side, her gloved hand laying on the pile of wood. She had called to her Grandma then, over and over, as if suddenly released from a trance. Grandma did not hear her; could not respond to her calls. She would not wake up and Ava began to cry.

After that Ava dreamed of her sometimes, but she could barely remember what happened. She could only recall Grandma Verna smiling and waving her gloved hand. She woke up night after night with tears on her cheeks.

Jenney was taking Ava to Grandpa's house to spend the night, as she had done a few times before. Ava was excited to visit Grandpa Harry, but she did not want to sleep over.

Grandpa was waiting for Jenney and Ava at the end of his short dirt road. He was waiting there to walk with her the rest of the way. Grandpa had his water bucket, so Ava knew they would have to walk down the side of the busy road to draw water before going on to Grandpa's house. They reached the place on the road and Grandpa stopped and lowered his bucket into the well-spring. The spring was almost completely hidden from view even though they were walking. The area surrounding the spring was covered by thin tree branches and leaves. Grass grew thick and tall all around. When the water bucket was filled, Grandpa used the attached rope to pull the water up and into view. They began their short trek back to the dirt road.

Walking the tree lined road was scary for Ava. The tall trees seemed to sway a hundred miles in the air. They all looked as though they were trying to reach out and grab her. Rabbits and squirrels would frequently dart from one side of the dirt road to the other, frightening the little girl. Grandpa would laugh and tell her not to worry. He said he would protect her.

Grandpa Harry seemed ancient to Ava. He wore blue denim coveralls that seemed to hitch up higher in the back. His head was a white patch of thick fuzz, curly and untamed. His dark brown skin was a startling contrast. Grandpa Harry was never seen without a pack of Red Man chewing tobacco sticking out of his coveralls front pocket, no doubt accounting for his missing teeth. He would spit out a dark stream of fragrant tobacco juice every few minutes. Still, he seemed a kindly gentleman, always willing to lend a helping hand to his family and neighbors. He did not have much, but he was quick to share what little he had.

As they reached the yard, Ava saw the tiny house her grandfather had lived in alone for years. The wood was old and knotted in places, the tin roof was thin and had many holes where leaks came through when it rained. Grandpa kept wide metal bowls on the floor to catch the water. The sound of the water splashing into the bowl was tinny and surreal. As they approached the backdoor, Ava wrinkled her nose at the oily smell of the old clothes washer and the noisy refrigerator sitting in the back room. There was a small bed with dirty, stained sheets as she walked through the barely attached backdoor. The fresh water went into a large, metal bowl which was kept uncovered, with a long-handled, faded silver dipper that everyone would either pour or drink from.

The living room area was cluttered. A wood encased floor model tv sat against a portion of the wall on the right. The space was narrow, linear with all items pushed to the left and right to create a small walkway through the center. Figurines stood small and large throughout the house. Most were cheap ceramic carvings of angels, gazing sorrowfully into space. There were others made to look like cats, dogs, and even pig shaped. The low ceiling made the cramped space feel claustrophobic. Ava was afraid to walk through the house alone.

The walkway continued, leading past the front door and into a dark, musty dining room. The large round table seemed massive in the small house, leaving no room for chairs. The table was littered with papers, dishes, and even more figurines. There were boxes of newspapers, magazines, old record albums and books. A thick layer of dust covered every single surface. The plain, coarse, wood walls contained dark blue pictures with sayings like, Bless This House. White Jesus looked ominously down from one of them. His blue eyes seemed to trail her every move, ever watchful, accusing, and formidable.

There was a bed past the table at the far end of the house. Grandpa Harry would put Ava to bed there at night. The dust would curl into the air when he placed her upon the bed, which was set high up off the floor. Heavy blankets covered the mattress and heavier quilts covered Ava, nearly choking her in her sleep.

That night, Ava could only move her head as she tried to see objects in the darkened room. Her arms were tucked at her sides, held tightly in place by the pile of quilts. Her vision was limited to a small sliver of light coming from the dim lamp in Grandpa Harry's room, just beyond the table near her bed. She could see his hands holding the Bible as he slowly leafed through the pages. Leaning his head back against the headboard, his face was hidden from her view. Ava felt trapped, weighed down by the heavy covers and the huge table that was too close to the bed. She had only to reach out with her little arm, if she could free it from the tightly tucked quilts, and she would be able to touch it. Ava could not see White Jesus looking down at her from his perch on the wall behind her, but she felt his gaze just the same. She usually took comfort from his image, but this house gave him an ominous feel. Ava could hear the noises outside, the frogs, crickets, and the rustling of grass as critters cut through nearby. She heard Grandpa Harry cough. She pulled the tight covers up over her mouth and tucked under as far as she dared. She heard him lay the Bible on the table holding the lamp. The sound carried as his bare feet found the cold wood floor. Ava peeked out from her dusty refuge and saw Grandpa Harry's white hair haloed from the dim light behind him as he walked slowly to the doorway. As he came through, Ava tucked her face completely under the heavy quilts and willed herself to sleep.

Ava woke up cold, wet, and terrified. The room was shrouded in near darkness, the only light coming through a crack in the rough wood wall. She remembered Grandpa putting her to bed the night before, but somehow, she had awakened in his bed. There was a puddle underneath her and she knew she had wet herself during the night. Shivering and alone, Ava began to cry. The smell of his private parts permeated the room, the sheets, her clothes, and her tiny hands. Flashes of his blue denim coveralls on the floor ran inexplicably through her mind. Ava could not remember what had happened. She did not know how she got into Grandpa Harry's bed. She felt wrong and confused and just wanted her mom to come back for her.

CHAPTER 2
THE MORNING AFTER

Grandpa came rushing into the room at the sound of Ava's crying. He called to her and told her she would need to get a move on. Ava felt a shiver, a violent shudder run through her at the sound of his voice, and she cried harder. A moment later he was pulling her from the bed, rushing her to get cleaned up and dressed. "Your mama will be here soon, so we have to take our walk now," he said.

Grandpa took Ava to the little room at the other end of the house. Ava stared down at her feet as they slowly made their way across the creaking floor. Each step felt precarious, as though the wood might splinter under her feet. Once they reached the tiny room, Grandpa made her stand still while he took off her top. Ava obediently raised her arms, still sniffling. She put her arms down and tried to cross them in front of her, to hide herself from the cold and his piercing eyes. He told her to lift her leg, one by one, as he removed her wet pajamas and underwear. Ava squeezed her eyes shut and did as she was told. Grandpa had warmed some water on the wood burning stove in the kitchen. He used a filthy rag to soap Ava's tiny little frame. He washed her roughly and quickly and rinsed the towel in the warm water. Ava stood shivering as he wiped the soap from her. He paused slightly when the towel reached between her thighs. Ava opened her eyes and squeezed her legs shut. Grandpa Harry hurriedly finished removing the soap. He dressed her in fresh clothes.

The two began their walk from his small yard hidden at the end of the short, tree-lined dirt road. Grandpa Harry walked faster than usual and bade Ava come along. He held out his forefinger for her to hold onto as they reached the highway. The tiny country store was to the right and less than a quarter mile. Still, traffic was always coming through and an errant child could easily get run over. Once they reached the little country store, grandpa held the door open and helped Ava over the steep step leading inside. He told her to choose any three items. He bought himself an RC Cola.

Grandpa and Ava had just made it back to the small house as Mama drove into the yard. Ava ran to the car and hopped in while her mom held the door open. As soon as she got in, she lay on the front seat beside Mama and began to cry silently. Mama put the car into gear and began driving. It was a few minutes before little Ava stopped crying to herself and sat up to look out of the window. She was feeling sad, but she did not know why. As they drove, she saw the little white house across the street from Grandpa's road where her daddy's cousin lived. Further along, she saw the big white house with all the horses and the huge fields of corn Carl sometimes bought from the tall white man that owned it all. Soon, they turned down a tiny paved road that would take them closer to home. They passed the house where Mama's white friend Sandy lived and the office for the paper mill on the right. That was where the pavement ended, and they entered the Quarters- the dirt road where all the black people lived.

Mama took Ava inside and gave her a bath in the sparse bathroom of their large, rented house. Ava shivered as Jenney poured the lukewarm water over her little body. The soapy water stung when it ran over her private area. Ava whimpered when Mama began washing her there. Mama said, "show me where it hurts, Ava." Ava pointed to her private area. Mama asked if she had fallen and hurt herself there and Ava said no. "It hurt when I woke up, Mama," whispered Ava, with her eyes downcast. Without another word, Mama dressed her and left the room.

It would be the first of many family secrets.

CHAPTER 3
SUNDAY SCHOOL

Jenney and Carl got Ava dressed and took her to church nearly every Sunday. Jenney would cook a big breakfast of homemade biscuits, grits, eggs, and ham. Little Ava loved her mama's cooking. She wished she did not get full so quickly. She would try to choke down every single bite. Mama had told her some kids did not have enough food every day and it was wasteful to throw hers away. Besides, Ava wanted to hurry up and get to church.

The church was down an unpaved, grassy path close to the house they lived in. Cars had to go slowly over the bumpy road. The church was a small, white structure made of wood and without heat or air conditioning. Summers were blazing hot inside the building and winters were freezing cold. Luckily, the month of April had been mild. The small congregation was made of up black and white members, which was odd for a small Alabama town. Chatom was not known for being the most enlightened place. With a dollar store, a small grocery, and a pharmacy, the town was not exactly booming. There was a small motel at the center of town and the courthouse was across the railroad track. The schools were further down the main street. Most of the town's people separated themselves along racial lines and did not attempt to mix. Still, the members of Ava's church family were closely knit and worked hard to maintain their congregation.

The railroad track became a trestle bridge that trailed across a narrow running stream near the church property. Only a small number of trains ever came through that way. After church, Ava would run after the older kids along the track. They would throw rocks into the stream below.

Ava would sometimes hear Jenney and Carl talking about their life in the church. It seemed that her parents loved God and hated things that were sinful. Ava learned that smoking, drinking alcohol, and saying bad words were sins. The preacher said people doing those things would go to hell. She was confused about that because her parents smoked and drank and used "bad words" all the time.

Ava loved going to church and learning the stories her teachers taught her about God and Jesus. She learned quickly and was always eager to hear more. Ava particularly liked the story of Lazarus and how Jesus raised him from the dead. Jenney would read to her at home too, so she would not forget. Her Sunday school teachers told her about the importance of being kind and helpful to others. They said Jesus had set examples by visiting those who were sick and shut in. Since being shut in meant they could not leave their homes, it was important to visit them to make sure they were well.

At the age of three, Ava memorized the 23rd Psalm. Jenney and Carl were so amazed that she could recite it all the way through. They told members of the church and the preacher asked them to let Ava come to the front and show what she had learned. In her cute little girl voice, Ava recited the Psalm, just as she had learned it. She knew some of the words by sight, after the nights she had spent watching Jenney read from the Bible. It was not hard for Ava to recall them and she was not afraid. Everyone said Ava was a smart little girl as they congratulated her parents on a job well done. Ava did not know it yet, but the seeds of her faith had been sown.

Ava soon grew to forget the things that had happened with her Grandpa as time went on. She spent the next several years enjoying being a little kid. She became friends with a girl from the quarters, Lynette. Ava spent most of her time playing hide-and-go-seek with her friend and trying to beat her when they raced. Lynette was always a little faster, but Ava did not mind. Lunch times were often spent on Lynette's back porch. Even though he was a little scary, Lynette's dad always made them sandwiches and Kool-Aid. Lynette was her best friend even though she could be mean at times. Once she had told Ava to go home because Ava would not stop singing. Ava thought that was mean, but Lynette did not like her singing church songs. Ava's mom said it was ok because best friends sometimes disagreed. She knew her mom was right because Lynette made her laugh a lot too. Ava just tried to remember not to sing around Lynette.

CHAPTER 4
SINS OF THE FATHER

Jenney was almost 31 years old the summer of 1982 and still slender with smooth caramel colored skin. She took care with her appearance, so her hair was always neatly done in the latest styles. For a while she sported a natural before getting a Jheri Curl. She wore that style for years and finally began straightening her shoulder length hair with a relaxer. Jenney favored wearing jeans and loose blouses that hugged her in the right places. Jenney was quite attractive. There was never a shortage of men vying for her attention, despite the fact she was married.

Jenney had met and married her first husband when she was almost 17. Jenney said it was love at first sight. She was devastated when after only two years, her husband had an accident at a lake and drowned. Jenney later gave birth to a son, Jimmy in 1969 and allowed her mother to raise him. Jimmy would come to visit his mom on occasion, mostly when school was out for the summer. Ava thought her brother was the best. She always looked forward to his visits because he was never too busy to play outside with her.

Jenney had met and married Carl and soon found herself

in a toxic situation. She began drinking early on. Jenney had grown up watching her father drink, so the habit was easy to pick up. She was soon known as a party girl. She always seemed to have music going and she was not afraid to dance. Even at home she and Carl smoked weed with their friends several times a week. Partying together seemed to cause more problems and the evenings often ended with Carl hitting Jenney again. As the beatings seemed to occur more frequently, so did Jenney's drinking.

Eight-year-old Ava was on the playground when the teacher came for her. Mrs. Bryce had said her mother was there to pick her up and that it seemed urgent. Ava was immediately scared. Ava's sister Elena, five years old, was waiting in the old blue Ford pick-up truck with their mama. The two little girls had to share a seat, since the middle part was taken up by the big hump in the floor. Jenney started the truck, pulled out into traffic, and sped quickly down the straight, paved highway.

They had not gone more than a few miles outside of town when Jenney started cursing at the slow-moving vehicle in front of them. She moved into the other lane to pass. It was then that Ava noticed the hill they were approaching and the bottle of J.W. Dant sitting between her mama's thighs. The rest happened so fast; it was hard for Ava to remember it all in sequence. A car topped the hill, Jenney panicked and cut hard to the right to avoid a head on collision with it. The rear of the old truck smacked the front bumper of the car she had been passing, causing them to swerve off the road. The blue pick-up weaved, trembled, and almost stalled out before pitching into the same ditch as the car they had just run off the road. Jenney maneuvered the stubborn old truck back up the grassy shoulder, spinning and sliding. She fought with the wheel until the truck relented, the slick tires gaining purchase and finally finding the street. She left the scene still cursing.

What Happens in the Family | 15

Jenney was not having a good day. She could barely stand as she staggered out of the truck and ushered the two girls into the big, creepy house. She sent both girls to the room they all slept in and ordered them to gather clothes. She said that Carl was a no-good, lying, cheating son-of-a-bitch and she was leaving him. As an inebriated Jenney stormed around the house grabbing random items to take to Grandma's house, Carl came home. Jenney went running and screaming at him and he slapped her hard across the face. Ava and Elena screamed as she fell to the floor. Jenney scrambled to her feet and began screaming at Carl again. This time he slapped her hard across the other side of her face. Carl half shoved, and half carried Jenney to the bedroom and locked the door. The screams continued as the 5'9" two hundred fifty-pound man unleashed his rage on his wife. Carl was a terrifying menace when he was fired up. It was always scary when he got like this, but he had never beaten Jenney this badly before. Ava and Elena shouted and screamed every time they heard another 'thwack,' against their mama's body. The girls beat on the locked door and begged Carl to let them inside. "Please stop hitting her," they yelled. Jenney was screaming from inside the room. Helpless squeals, and pitiful howls sounded with each landed blow. Through it all, Carl never uttered a sound.

Finally, the screaming stopped. The room was silent for long moments. Both girl's faces were drenched in tears, snot running from their noses. They shook and trembled with fear, wondering why their mama was so quiet in there. Ava whispered, "Daddy, can we come in?" Carl did not reply. Elena cried, calling for her mama repeatedly, but Carl still said nothing. There was silence all around. The girls wrapped their arms around each and sat on the floor next to the bedroom door. Hours passed.

The girls were awakened by the sound of the bedroom door screeching open. Not waiting for permission, the two sisters ran into the bedroom searching for their mom. They found her on the bed she shared with Carl. She was curled into a ball, crying softly, and moaning in pain. Her face was swollen and bloody and she had cuts above one eye. Her nose did not look quite right, and blood dribbled from it onto her chest. Ava went to the bathroom and wet a towel to help clean her mama's face. As she climbed up onto the bed and began dabbing at the worst of the wounds, Ava noticed Carl glowering at them through the doorway. Elena curled up beside her mama while Ava tended her wounds. Carl left them that way and drove off in his 1976 Oldsmobile 98.

CHAPTER 5
NEAR DEATH

A few weeks later, Ava and Elena were playing hide and go seek outside in the front yard. The yard was large and had plenty of big oak trees that offered easy hiding spaces. The day was pretty, but it was approaching summer and temperatures were in the upper 80's. Every now and then a gentle breeze would stir up the sand in the middle of the yard. The sisters would laugh and giggle even when hiding, giving away the game. Jenney had made them some fresh iced tea earlier in the day, and the girls were thirsty. Ava and Elena chased each other up the steps to the old house in search of their mama and the tea.

The house was old, big, and creepy. The paint on the old wood was faded all around, but you could tell it once was white. Someone had trimmed the windows in blue, but that had long since peeled away leaving only the slightest traces. The porch stretched from end to end on the front of the house, but the rails would give you splinters if you were careless. The house was divided into cavernous rooms including a living room with two long windows that went almost to the high ceiling. The kitchen had plenty of space and the girls often ran in and out of the back door set off to the right. There were three huge bedrooms in the house and one equally spacious bathroom. Wood floors ran the length of the entire house. There was no insulation. Midnight trips to the bathroom during winter were freezing cold and frantic.

Neighborhood kids made fun and said the house was haunted. A man had gone crazy and shot his wife, killing her in the back bedroom. The stories said the dead woman's blood would show through the wood on rainy days. No one slept in that room. Carl and Mama shared a bed that was pushed to the wall on the right side of the first bedroom. All the rooms had doorways connecting each subsequent area. The only access to the other two was through the first room. The girls' bed was pushed against the wall on the left side of the same room Jenney and Carl slept in.

That is where they found Jenney. She was lying on her back, passed out on the floor beside the girls' bed. Ava thought she had drunk too much whiskey again, so she wet a towel and began washing Jenney's face to try to wake her up. That usually did the trick. This time, Jenney would not wake up. She moaned and grabbed for her stomach, so weak her arms fell to her sides. The girls became scared. Ava ordered Elena to stay with their mom and she ran across the dirt road to get help from their neighbors, the Walton's. Ava was banging on their door within minutes. Jefferey was the only one home. "What's wrong with Jenney, Ava, what are you going on about?" Ava told Jefferey that Jenney was passed out and would not wake up. Jefferey went back inside the house and called for an ambulance. Ava asked if she could use the phone to call the office for the mill. She needed Carl to come home and help Jenney. Jefferey let her use the phone, and Ava dialed the number from memory. As soon as she hung up, she and Jefferey ran across the road to check on her mom.

Carl was home before the ambulance showed up. He came

What Happens in the Family | 19

inside barking orders, yelling at the girls to back away from Jenney and get out of the room. He yelled at Jefferey to get the hell out of his house and promised to deal with him later. Carl then dropped to the floor and carefully lifted Jenney's head onto his lap. He called to her repeatedly, but she would only moan feverishly. A grunt of pain escaped Jenney's lips every few seconds. Finally, the ambulance arrived outside, along with half the neighborhood. They trickled down the dirt road soon after they heard the squealing ambulance arrive. After realizing what was happening one of the older women corralled the two sisters and took them home with her. They would not see Mama or Carl again for days.

Carl came and picked them up on the third day. The girls had been well cared for by Aunt Eliza, who was not really their aunt. All the neighborhood kids called her that. She made them tea cakes and read them Bible verses each night. Carl told the girls they were going to Mobile to see their Mama at the hospital. They were excited to see Mama, but the girls knew this meant they would get to eat at McDonald's like all the other times they had gone to Mobile. The drive took just over an hour and the girls fell asleep. When they woke up, Carl was handing them their Big Macs and fries. As always, Carl made them slow down enough to bless the food. The girls ripped into the cartons and devoured the burgers in minutes.

They reached the hospital shortly after. Carl took them inside. The halls were wide, white floors all around, and the walls were a pale, dull brown. Ava hated the smells but wanted to see her mom. Carl led them up the stairs and finally down a long hall to Jenney's room. She was sitting up in bed drinking something from a straw. The girls ran inside and leaped for Jenney, both eager for the reunion. Jenney grabbed each of them and gave them hugs and kisses. Carl left the room.

Mama looked weak but her voice held a note of strength. Her bruises from the beating she took weeks ago had faded at least. Mama explained that she had been carrying a baby, but she lost it. Elena thought the baby must have been stolen, but Mama told her no and tried to explain. She said the baby had been growing in the wrong place inside her body and a rupture had occurred. The rupture caused her to bleed inside and the doctors had to perform surgery to help her. She said the doctors explained that her heart had stopped beating for several minutes during the operation, but the doctor kept shocking her to bring her back. Mama said she was thankful for the doctors because they had saved her life. She told the girls to add an extra special prayer of thanks when they said their prayers for the night.

CHAPTER 6
BROTHERLY LOVE

Mama came home from the hospital a week later, at the end of July 1982. She had arranged for Jimmy, her son from her first marriage to come stay with them and help around the house. Jimmy lived with their grandma Nancy, in Choctaw County Alabama about an hour away, in the opposite direction of Mobile. She had raised him since Jenney was so young when she had him.

Jimmy was thirteen and already had an eye for girls. He would talk about them all the time. Ava guessed that Jimmy never really thought about anything else, because that was all he ever wanted to talk about. Jimmy was around six feet and he was not nearly finished growing yet. People were already calling him tall. His short afro was thick and so sandy it earned him the nickname Red. He liked to play basketball and according to him he was quite good. Jimmy was also good at drawing and he loved to show off his work. Her brother would brag that he had all the talent and the looks in the family.

Jimmy put the groceries away and helped Mama to her bed. Elena was in the Quarters playing with her friend Cassie. Carl was out. Jimmy told Ava he had to watch her since Mama was asleep and he took her into the back bedroom that no one ever used. The bedroom shared a wall with Mama's room and the walls were very thin. Jimmy began telling her about two girls that he liked. He said they wanted him to choose. Ava was bored and not paying attention. She tried to stifle a yawn. Her breathing began to grow steady and even as she lay there listening to her brother tell her stories about girls, drawing, and music. It all sounded so boring to her and she could not imagine why he thought she would care. Still, she wanted to be polite, but her thoughts kept drifting off. Jimmy's voice took on a surreal quality, seeming farther and farther away.

Ava could not remember falling asleep, but when she woke up her brother had his fingers in her underwear. She could feel his hard fingers jabbing in and out of her body. His nails were scraping her insides. The pain took her breath away, making her head swim. She was scared and could not make sense of what was happening.

She pushed at his hand and told him to stop, but he grabbed her shoulder and held her in place. Ava cried out, still pushing at Jimmy's hand, and trying to squirm away from his grasp. Jimmy removed his hand from Ava's underwear and pushed her hard into the bed. He rolled onto her and began grinding his penis into her crotch, fully clothed. He whispered to her harshly, telling her to be quiet. Ava beat at his shoulders, pushing and squirming trying to move his weight off her. Jimmy seemed to like that. He kept grinding into her, pushing her down into the mattress. She could feel the mattress springs pressing roughly into her back. She pushed at Jimmy's neck with her small hands, but he seemed to like that too. His face contorted and with a loud, guttural growl, he rolled off his little sister. Ava lay there stunned and dazed for a heartbeat. Too shocked to cry, she was not sure what her brother had just done to her. She felt scared and stupid. This was not supposed to happen. He was supposed to be her protector. This did not make any sense. She sat up to leave the bed and Jimmy shoved her face into the wall. Ava began to cry quietly. "Get out crybaby," he said. Ava scrambled down off the bed and left the room. She never told a soul.

That night Ava prayed that God would forgive her for whatever she had done to cause her brother to hurt her. She hoped her brother was not mad. Ava decided she would forgive Jimmy because that was what she was supposed to do. She wanted him to go back to the way he used to be, nice, sweet, and protective. She knew that if she told anyone, her brother would be in trouble and she did not want to cause him any problems. Now that she was thinking it through, Ava knew her brother must be sorry for what he had done and was just waiting for her to make amends.

Ava did not see Jimmy again until the end of September. She came home from school and there he was, sitting on the sofa drinking a glass of iced tea. Ava felt her cheeks get warm when she saw him sitting there. Until then, she did not realize she was angry. She would usually run to give Jimmy a big hug, this time she walked right past. She did not look his way again, and quickly found an excuse to leave the house. She walked the path to the church and followed the train tracks. She sat down on the trestle bridge, her legs dangling over the side. She sat there throwing rocks into the little creek, wasting as much time as she could, but her thoughts kept returning to him. She decided she was better off staying away from him as much as possible. She did not want to take a chance. She was not going to rat him out because she knew he would get in trouble. She would just stay silent about it. She would keep his dirty secret.

CHAPTER 7
LOVE THY NEIGHBOR

Ava walked slowly down the dirt road, digging her heels deep into the warm, red sand. Mid October temperatures were a relief from the previous summer's heat. Mama insisted she must take a plate of food to the paraplegic man under the hill. His name was Wesley, and he lived in a house all alone. His two older sisters lived just down the way but paid for his living expenses so that he could have his own place. They had hired a nurse to come look after him several days a week. Ava sometimes helped in the kitchen to prepare meals for Mr. Wesley on the days the nurse was there. She liked those days. On other days, like today, Jenney would send a plate of food to make sure he had something to eat.

The house was pale green, all wood, with no insulation. There were two bedrooms in the house and an exceptionally large kitchen. The living room served as Wesley's convalescent space. There were precious few furnishings, save a couple of plastic chairs near the bed. A television had been set up on the wall across from the bed, so that the resident patient had to look up to view. One window that faced the front, right next to the entrance, housed an old air conditioning unit, to battle the stifling Alabama heat.

Mr. Wesley spent his days and nights bound to the oversized hospital bed that jutted out into the middle of the room. Ava felt sorry for him. She could not imagine having to live in that bed all day every day. She would add him to her nightly prayer.

The living room smelled of medication, ointment, and urine. Mr. Wesley's handheld urinal sat on the brown table right next to his bed, emptied of its previous contents. Ava knew she would be expected to give it to him for his use and empty it once again when he finished. She was not looking forward to that.

Though his lower half was paralyzed, Mr. Wesley had great upper body strength. He could pull himself into a sitting position and use his arms to propel himself backwards to a degree. His arms seemed longer than they should have been. His fingers seemed to curl almost to his wrists.

Ava tried to be as helpful as she could. He called her over and asked her to help him sit up. He needed to use the urinal, he told her and could not do that lying down. He was always clothed in a thin hospital gown with the traditional opening in the back. His musky scent permeated the bed and the room. Ava found herself gagging at the competing odors. Still, she dipped her little shoulder and allowed the paraplegic man to encircle her with his arms to pull himself up and onto the side of the bed. His useless feet had no problem reaching the floor, as he had long legs, even if they no longer worked. His gown worked its way up as he repositioned. Once he was sitting, Ava stepped back and reached for the empty urinal and held it for his grasp. He took it. That is when she discovered that Mr. Wesley had the strength of an ox in his hands and arms.

He grabbed her so fast, she failed to see the danger until it was too late. He pulled her to him and fastened his crusty lips onto her mouth. He had long since lost his teeth, and his gums looked disgusting to her. His breath smelled hot and nasty, like he had been eating tuna hours before. She tried to pull away, to run, but he held her arms in his iron-like grip. His nails were long and hard, and dug deeply into her skin. He moved his mouth away from hers but did not release his grip on Ava's arm. He moved his hands up slightly and roughly pushed her head down to his lap, forcing her face into his crotch. No longer holding the urinal, Wesley grabbed his long, thick, limp penis and attempted to shove into Ava's closed mouth. Ava gritted her teeth; she squeezed her eyes tightly shut as she furiously turned her head from side to side. She could feel the wet tip of his penis brushing hard against her lips.

"Just kiss it, Ava. It won't bite," said Mr. Wesley. She could hear his lecherous grin as he spoke. Ava felt nausea build quickly as the bile rose into her throat. She swallowed it back down to keep from opening her mouth, knowing what he would do. Ava squealed through closed lips, as Wesley continued to hold onto her. Her bony arms flailed in the air, hitting, and pushing against his unfeeling legs, to no avail. Despite her efforts to keep her mouth closed, she could now taste Wesley's sweat, musk, and urine on her lips. She struggled harder and twisted herself around. As she did, she saw a face at the window. The nurse! Someone who could help her. She squealed again, this time out loud and Wesley's hand moved to cover her mouth. With her back to him, he was so busy trying to make her comply, he never looked toward the window.

Ava begged for help with her eyes firmly latched onto the nurse's gaze. The woman reached for the door, moving away from the window, but in the next instant she peeked inside the house once again. She brought both hands to the glass and put her face on the windowpane. She looked right into Ava's terrified eyes, saw her twisting and trying to get away, heard her muffled squeals. Ava watched through terrified eyes as the nurse turned and walked away.

Ava lost her mind to fear. She became wild, furiously turning and twisting, and trying to wrench free of the terrifying vise holding her captive. She opened her mouth beneath his fingers and bit down as hard as she could. Wesley howled in pain, forgetting to hold onto his prey. Blood spurt onto Ava's lips. Panicked, Ava ran to the door, wrenched it open and sprinted towards the dirt road. As she ran, she sobbed loudly, tears blinded her, and she angrily wiped them with the back of her hand. Snot ran down her nose, and she wiped that with the back of her white t-shirt.

As she ran towards her house, she saw the nurse at the neighbor's house across the road. She ran right past her, not even wondering what they were saying about her. So incensed and terrified, Ava was convinced the paralyzed man was on her heels, and she dared not look back. She tripped over a rock and fell to the ground, cutting her knees. Her shorts were little protection against the hard pebbles in the dirt and the cuts stung immediately. Convinced he would catch her soon, Ava scrambled to her feet, her terrified thoughts irrational, but propelling her steadily onward. Now limping, she realized her ankle was hurt, but she refused to stop moving. She limped as quickly as she could, feeling her heart pound heavily.

She got home with dirt in her long dark ponytails and under her fingernails. Mama saw what a mess she was, with blood on her knees, snot on her nose and dirty tears streaking her face. She reached out for her daughter, but Ava ignored her. She ran to the bathroom and ran the cold water. She jumped into the bathtub before the water had even covered the bottom. Ava grabbed the towel next to the tub and began to scrub her face and her hands. She could not get the scent of him off her and she could still smell his breath on her lips. She gargled with the water from the faucet trying to rinse his blood from her mouth. She shivered in the cold water and did not even notice. She thought she would never feel clean again.

After a few long moments, Jenney entered the bathroom. She sat on the side of the tub and asked Ava "what is wrong?" Ava just stared into space, holding her arms tight to her body. "Did somebody hurt you, beat you up, you look a mess right now?" Ava never replied. Jenney said "well, I'm here if you decide to tell me," and she wandered slowly from the room. She pulled the bathroom door closed as she left.

Ava wondered if she had done the right thing. Her mom had asked her what happened, but she was too ashamed to tell. She thought she had done something to make these things keep happening to her. The things that had occurred were not her mother's fault. She would apologize for being rude to her in the morning. She should not have gotten so close to him and he would not have done those terrible things. Ava knew that if she ever told, no one would believe her anyway. She wondered briefly about the nurse who saw. Why had she run away? Ava thought it was because the nurse knew it was Ava's fault, not Mr. Wesley's. Ava felt deeply ashamed. She was supposed to be helpful and kind to others, but she had failed. She would work extra hard to be a better person and things were going to be fine.

Ava whispered her prayers until she felt calm enough to fall asleep.

CHAPTER 8
IT TAKES A VILLAGE

By the summer of 1983, Ava was beginning to change. She had endured so much pain during her short nine years that it opened her eyes to just how ugly life could be. She tried not to let her guard down around others, but she continued to pray and ask God for forgiveness for her sins. She felt that she was being punished for something she had done, so she tried to be a good girl. She spent her time at school paying attention to her teachers and getting good grades and racing the other girls at recess. She did not talk back when her parents gave her instructions, she always did as she was told. She helped her mother with the chores in the house, even without being asked. Even though her parents did not take her to church as often as before, Ava continued to read her Bible most days. It comforted her to know that God was watching over her even when the adults in her life were not.

Jenney had recently developed a habit of sending Elena to play with Cassie and having Ava walk up the long dirt road to stay with Mama's friend Sandy. Ava walked barefoot alone, without fear because she knew Sandy's house was right past the office and the mill where Carl worked. The mill was under a hill on the other side of the road, so she could never quite make out Carl 's hard hat from where she walked along the street.

She walked past the mill and then the office and Sandy's house stood alone on the right. She knocked lightly on the front door and waited for Sandy to come to answer. Sandy was married, but Ava knew her husband Simon, was always away at work. Even though Sandy was white, Mama liked to hang out with her so they could smoke weed. They only did this at Mama's house though in case Simon came home early.

Sandy finally opened the door and greeted Ava with a bubbly air of welcome. She bent down and hugged the little girl and took her inside for a glass of Kool-Aid. Sandy showed her how to play tic-tac-toe and Ava thought that was neat. The phone in the kitchen trilled a loud, harsh ring and Sandy jumped to go answer. When she returned, she was slightly flushed and began gathering Ava's things. A few moments later a visitor arrived at the house. Ava accompanied Sandy out to the small front porch and saw there was a tall, skinny, white man standing in the yard next to his white Chevy pickup. He had brown, shaggy, hair and hair around his mouth and chin. He was not Mr. Simon. He asked Sandy "who's the kid?" Sandy said she was babysitting, but she really wanted to go on their drive. The man told her sure, just bring the kid with you if you want.

The man got back into his truck, then Sandy slid in next to him. She grabbed for Ava and closed the door after she was settled. Sandy put the greasy seat belt across Ava and buckled it, pulling it tight. The man started the truck and turned left, headed back towards the mill. Instead of taking the right that would lead back to the Quarters, he kept straight despite the road narrowing to a mere grassy path. They drove over bumps until they could no longer see the road behind them.

The man stopped the truck and cut the engine. Sandy

began to undress. She slid out of her short shorts and let them fall to the dirty truck floor. She began kissing the man on the lips, moaning as they embraced. Ava was scared. She tried to unbuckle the seatbelt and began silently, slowly reaching for the door handle. It was missing altogether. A silver screw stuck out from a small hole where the handle should have been. She tried to push herself as far into the passenger door as she could, to get away from the couple making out right next to her. Ava closed her eyes tight, trying to erase herself from her seat.

Sandy was making wet sounds as she began sucking the man's penis. She made sexual noises and the man thrust himself into her mouth repeatedly. The man whispered to Sandy and she shifted so that she was facing him. Though still under the steering wheel, he maneuvered to face her as well. Sandy began thrusting her lower half towards the man and Ava knew they were having sex. The white truck began to rock with their motion. The noises got louder and more impassioned, making Ava wish she could disappear.

The man whispered again, and Sandy turned to Ava. She said, "Ava this is Tim and he likes you a lot." The couple was still thrusting and grunting, having sex in the truck with Ava sitting next to them. Sandy told Ava to say "hi." Ava closed her eyes, turned her head, and pressed her forehead to the closed window of the passenger door. The couple sounds got louder. Sandy said, "Ava come here, Tim wants you to try it too." Ava shook her head, no and remained where she was. Sandy said, "don't say no, baby it feels so good, I promise." She let out another moan of pleasure as if to underscore her words and then reached for the little girl.

Ava squeezed her eyes shut again and held on tight to the seat belt even as Sandy unbuckled it. Sandy turned and began kissing Ava's tears and whispering, "please stop crying baby, I promise he won't hurt you." Sandy then picked Ava up and dragged her limp body across so that they switched places. Ava was now right next to the man. She could smell their mingled scents from their sex in the air of the small truck. Only the man's window was open, but Ava did not open her eyes to see. The man began placing kisses on Ava's forehead, telling her she was a pretty girl. He said he could make her feel good too if she would only stop crying. Ava sobbed loudly, her tiny body quaking with fear. Sandy pulled Ava's shorts and underwear down just enough to uncover her bottom. She began touching the little girl's private area while whispering, "shhh, sweet girl, it's ok."

Tim began rubbing his penis, priming himself again. Sandy slid closer to the passenger door, pulling Ava by the shoulders so she could lay her on the seat between her and Tim. Ava continued to sob. Tim pulled Ava's shorts the rest of the way off her small body. The man stretched and twisted so that he could access Ava. Sandy held her still as the man entered the child. He started slowly at first, as if he were offering her some sort of kindness. He ignored Ava's cries and pushed into her harder as he spilled his seed into her body. Ava was screaming, but Sandy was holding her hand over her mouth, muffling the sound. She kept telling herself "no, no, no this can't be real." Ava passed out from the pain and shock of what they were doing to her.

When Ava woke up, she was in excruciating pain. She felt like something was stuck inside of her private part. Something sticky was on her thighs. She felt tears on her face, running into her ears. She sat up then, realizing she was not in her bed with her sister. Her breath began coming in short, quick bursts and her head started to spin. Her stomach hurt and she felt her mouth fill with saliva. She rolled and fell from the bed just as she began to retch. She vomited the red Kool-Aid onto the floor. Ava got up and Sandy came into the room. A glance out the window revealed it was dark outside, the sun having already gone down. "I have to go home," Ava whimpered weakly. Sandy replied, "ok, Simon can take you home now, but first let's take you to the bathroom."

Ava bolted to the door and fumbled with the handle. Somehow, she wrenched the door open. She let herself out, running down the road in a flash. She ran all the way past the office, the mill and down the red dirt road. She forgot about the darkness as she ran, tears were streaming down her face. She did not feel the pain in her bare feet as they were scraped and punctured by small rocks. She ignored the ache in her body. Ava ran blindly, a wildness taking over her mind. She saw nothing. Felt nothing, as though she were numb all over.

Unable to tell how much time had passed, Ava found herself at home. She was not quite sure if she had come straight there. She had no memory of arriving in the big yard or of walking up the wooden steps. She did not recall opening the front door. Ava found herself standing in the living room. Sweat dripped from her forehead and into her eyes. She barely felt the burn, but she became aware of the pain. Ava went to the bathroom and ran water in to the tub. She undressed quickly but quietly careful not to wake her mother. Carl's car was not outside, so she knew he was not at home. She had passed Elena, asleep in their shared bed. Ava slowly got into the tub and let her tears mingle with the flowing water. As Ava sobbed quietly, she wondered how a God who genuinely loved her could allow this to happen to her. Hadn't she been hurt enough times already? It was as if all the other men who hurt her were just previews for the horror she had just undergone.

That night, Ava refused to pray. She knew with a cold certainty that people were just bad. Everyone had a hidden side that they did not allow others to see until it was too late. Their face looked the same as everyone else, but their inside face was monstrous. Ava felt that she must be extra careful to avoid the secret monsters. She would need to keep them away from Elena too, so she would have to keep her close. Deep inside Ava knew that even though the monsters were bad, she must be doing everything wrong because they kept finding her. She had thought that by pleasing God and being a good girl, she could keep the monsters away. Now God had left her too and she was all alone.

She crept into her mother's bed and curled up on the far side, careful not to get too close. She felt hot tears on her cheeks long into the night. She woke up suddenly, heart beating loudly in her ears. She was sweating and trembling as terror coursed through her veins. It took Ava a few moments to realize she had been dreaming. She could still feel the monster's breath on the back of her neck as it reached out for her.

Ava never told a soul.

CHAPTER 9
BROKEN VOWS

It was getting close to the end of the summer and the family was throwing a block party. Ava knew this was just an excuse because their house was a party house nearly every weekend. Jenney and Carl would invite some of their family and friends from outside the Quarters, but others just seemed to show up on their own. There was music, dancing, drinking, smoking and all the things the kids were not supposed to see. The adults gathered around playing cards with a lot of trash-talking going on. Beer cans and whiskey bottles were scattered over the yard and the house.

People were milling around in the yard, standing on the front porch smoking weed, sitting on the rails telling stories everywhere Ava looked. Food was spread all around the kitchen and people were coming and going with plate after plate. Jenney had spent the day making macaroni and cheese, potato salad, collard greens, dressing, and deviled eggs. Carl cranked up his barbecue pit and grilled tons of chicken, hot dogs, baby back ribs and hamburgers. Several neighbors showed up with pies, cakes, drinks, and paper plates. Some of the kids were running around the yard playing tag until it got dark. The grownups made them all come inside, and they were scattered throughout the house.

Ava was not interested in playing with the other kids. She never even went to Lynette's house anymore. At school, she stopped going out for recess and had nothing to say to her classmates. When it was time to go out, she would tell her teacher her tummy hurt and stay seated at her desk. Sometimes she could have the whole classroom all to herself if Mrs. Bryce went to join the others on the playground. Ava spent the time staring out the window, daydreaming or with her head down on her folded arms, pretending to sleep. She just did not want anyone to talk to her so she would not have to talk to them. Ava was afraid they would see her shame. At home, she stayed close to the house and watched.

The party was in full swing with everyone talking at once. Ava noticed that Jenney was not in the room. Carl must have noticed it at about the same time because he suddenly got up from the card table. Ava watched as he went through the bedroom door, looking for Jenney. He emerged several minutes later, alone. Carl went outside to continue his search, but still he came up empty. As long moments passed, Ava could see the waves of anger coming from Carl. Jenney was still not in the house. Carl left all the people sitting in his house and got into his car and left. Hours later he returned. Jenney was back at home and the two began a loud argument. People began to trickle out the front door. Ava could see that things were going to escalate, so she considered doing the same. Before she could make up her mind, Carl hit Jenney across the face, leaving her lip split open and bleeding. Jenney turned to walk into the other room, she never dared to return his blows, but Carl grabbed her by the hair. He pulled her into the bedroom and Ava heard him hit Jenney once again. Suddenly, the house was completely empty. People were getting into their cars driving or walking away. No one wanted to get involved in a family dispute. Besides, they knew Carl 's reputation. Carl and his older brothers were known as fighters, troublemakers, and hellraisers. They had frequent run-ins with Washington County police some years before. Carl and his brothers were known for quick trigger fingers, not hesitating to use a gun. There was no way anyone was going to step in and try to tell Carl what to do, especially not in his own house.

Ava could hear Carl yelling at Jenney, accusing her of fooling around with Jeffery. He said she was over at the neighbor's house while the party had been going on. Someone had told him he saw her head that way, but Jenney said that was not true. She insisted she had never been involved with Jeffery, but Carl did not believe her. Ava wanted to mention the lady she had seen Carl hugging and kissing the week before, but she knew better than to open her mouth. That woman had been at their house for the party tonight and Ava wondered if her mother knew. They argued and yelled late into the night. Ava and Elena finally fell asleep when the two settled down.

Several weeks later the same lady came home in the car with Jenney. She was short, with dark brown skin, and wore her hair in a thick natural. Her name was Sue, and she was a very pretty lady. She wore heels and short skirts all the time, so Ava thought she must be a prostitute. Ava had seen her at the parties with several different men, so that could have been the truth. Ava decided she did not like this Sue, and she wanted her to go.

Later that evening, Jenney told the girls to make the bed in the back room. Sue was not leaving, in fact, she needed a place to stay. Since Jenney was her best friend, she decided to offer her the back room. She told Ava to go put some water on the stove to boil. When she was done, Jenney told her to take it into the back bedroom. Ava grabbed a big towel and grabbed the hot pot of water from the stove. She walked carefully, trying not to spill. She finally made it to the bedroom and sat the hot pot onto the wood floor. She reached out to open the door to the room and turned to retrieve the pot. Ava's mouth dropped open when she saw Sue lying on the floor. She was naked from the waist down, with the big red balloon thing Jenney kept hanging on the wall now laying flat between her legs. There was a long white cord laying next to the red bag. Ava had always wondered what that was for and she knew she was about to find out. She watched as Sue grabbed the red bag and unscrewed a cap Ava had never even noticed. She told Ava to pour the water into the opening. Ava's hands were shaking, but she did as Sue had instructed. She tried not to splash the water. The bag now slightly filled, Sue poured vinegar in and began to screw in the long white hose. She gave the bag a squeeze to mix the ingredients. Sue sat quietly for a few moments and Ava did not speak. She got up to leave, but Sue said "where do you think you're going girl? You have to help me with this." Ava looked around the room, suddenly feeling trapped. Sue checked the bag again and appeared to be satisfied that the water was now cooled. She motioned Ava to come closer. She walked over to Sue and watched until she saw what she was about to do. Sue grabbed the slotted end of the white tubing and inserted it into her vagina. Ava quickly averted her gaze as she took a step back. Sue told her to stop being a big baby and push down on the bag. Ava approached again, timidly. She sat down on her knees near the bag, positioned between Sue's legs. She gently pushed and the water began to flow. Soon there was a puddle covering the bare floor, running towards Ava's knees. Ava quickly adjusted her position and continued to press on the bag. She hoped it would empty soon.

Ava finished her task and left the room, but the image of

Sue lying on the bare floor refused to leave her mind. She would never let anyone make her do that again.

A FEW WEEKS had gone by and Sue was still in the house. Ava was tired of seeing her. She had figured out that Sue was not a nice woman. She would snap at Ava when Jenney was not in the room. She knew this lady was bad news. Ava saw her roll her eyes at her mom when Jenney was not looking, and she knew that was a bad sign. She guessed she would have to wait until her mom got tired of her.

School was still out, so Ava spent most of her days wandering around, trying to find secret places to hide. She wanted to be left alone. She found a spot, just beside the mill where her father worked. A few steps off the path to the church was an old abandoned house. There were some shaded places there to keep her cool while she sat thinking. Ava was always thinking. She had been at her spot for several hours and realized she was thirsty. Ava made her way back down the hill. When she got closer to the house, she heard yelling coming from the front porch.

Ava ran the rest of the way and stopped in her tracks as she came upon the scene. Jenney had Sue by her hair, and she was dragging her to the steps. She was punching and hitting her in the head and face. Sue was screaming and trying to get a grip on Jenney's hands, her bare feet kicking and making a running motion against the floor. Ava yelled, "mama what are you doing, you're hurting her?" Jenney screamed breathlessly "good that's what I want and that's what this bitch deserves!" Jenney began pounding Sue's face viciously as she dragged her to the steps. She turned around and pushed Sue the rest of the way. Ava stared in shock as Sue tumbled down the unforgiving steps. She landed at the bottom with a loud "whoof" as the air rushed from her lungs. Ava watched as Sue slowly got to her feet. Her strapless crop top had slipped upwards and now rested on her neck, baring her small breasts. She yanked it back into place. Jenney and Sue exchanged insults, still yelling at each other. Carl was watching from the doorway. That was when Ava understood.

CHAPTER 10
FAMILY TRADITIONS

A few days before school began again in 1983, the family was on the move. Carl and Jenney were going to visit Jenney's aunt Rosa in Melvin, Alabama and the girls were along for the trip. The drive took about an hour and the family usually spent the night when they went there.

Aunt Rosa was the older sister to Jenney's father. Although she appeared ancient to Ava and Elena, no one could deny she was a beautiful woman. Her skin was nearly white. She wore her hair short and always dyed some shade of blonde. No doubt she was one of those who could pass easily in her early years. Though born and raised in the heart of the south, Aunt Rosa spent her young adulthood in Chicago, Illinois. She had six children including a set of twin girls, all of whom she raised there. She brought her children back to the south. Rumors were that she had spent years in prison for murdering her husband.

She was still living in the family home where all her brothers and sisters had been raised. She was different than Ava's other aunts. She seemed to be angry every time they went to visit her. She drank and smoked like a chimney. She could drink more whiskey than the men who frequented her house. She had been known to have contests with some of them who probably regretted it later.

Despite an overwhelming sense of fear when she was near her, Ava and Aunt Rosa seemed to share a bond. Aunt Rosa would read Ava's fortune with her special cards on quiet mornings after everyone else had gone home. Still, the air of haughtiness, mystery, and power resonated off Aunt Rosa in waves. Ava fully believed her when she said she could see into the future and commune with the spirits of the dead.

Aunt Rosa ran a gambling operation in her home, and it was often filled with men and women from all around. She sold beer and whiskey and had dice games and cards set up where people played for money. She set the rules of the house and the winners had to share their money with her. It was the price of entry and the cost of gambling at her place. Aunt Rosa sold hot plates of food, so no one ever went hungry at her place. The catfish was Ava's favorite because Aunt Rosa made sure to fry hers with crunchy edges and she gave her extra fried okra.

The crowd of people would grow as the evenings wore on. Cars would line up along the long dirt road that led to Aunt Rosa's house. The drinking would increase along with the volume of the music playing inside. The kids were remanded to one room of the house so as not to disturb the grown- ups.

Bored, Ava and Elena had fallen asleep long before the music died down. Jenney would normally let them stay that way and they would leave in the morning. This time, Jenney came and shook both girls awake and told them to gather their things. Ava stumbled around over other sleeping children and did as she was told. As they left the room at the back of the small house, the sound of shouting and cursing jolted Ava fully awake. During the few steps it had taken them to reach the front porch, Ava could tell her Aunt Rosa was having one of

What Happens in the Family | 43

her violent meltdowns. She rubbed the remaining sleep from her eyes.

Aunt Rosa was drunk, staggering, sputtering at a giant of a man. He was at least 6'9" and weighed close to four hundred pounds. Ava knew him only as "Big Man," and as Aunt Rosa's live in boyfriend. The two had been a couple for a few years. Big Man was always kind to Ava and seemed to have a gentle soul. Ava had decided you never know about people, and she never allowed herself too close to the giant, just in case.

Aunt Rosa was brandishing a large kitchen knife and advancing on Big Man. As she came closer, she let loose a chorus of expletives. Ava did not know what had caused this, but she had witnessed similar scenes before and knew it did not take very much. Aunt Rosa was easily angered, and her temper was infamous in the community. Big Man was moving steadily backwards as Aunt Rosa advanced with the knife held out in front of her. Ava's dad was trying to calm Aunt Rosa down, but she turned and snarled at him. Carl pushed into the driver's seat of the car and told Jenney to get in too. Jenney pushed the girls into the car first, then slammed the back door shut.

As Jenney slipped into the front seat, Aunt Rosa suddenly lunged at Big Man. Her knife came away bloody. A bloody slice opened across his massive belly and through his collared shirt. Aunt Rosa was not yet done. She lunged again, this time catching Big Man in the face, slicing his cheek open deeply. Big Man seemed to barely register the cuts, even though they were open and oozing profusely. He continued calmly trying to talk to Aunt Rosa trying to decrease her rage. He stopped backing away and reached out to try to embrace her. The knife swiped his arm before she savagely pierced his right side. Big Man cried out, but still did not seem concerned with his growing number of wounds. He was still trying to calm Aunt Rosa.

Carl began to reverse the vehicle, his family still watching the events unfolding within the car's headlights. As he reversed,

Aunt Rosa dropped the knife. She reached out and grabbed for Big Man as though she were going to hug him. Relieved and no doubt believing her rage was finally spent, Big Man accepted her embrace. The couple hugged for a moment. Aunt Rosa released him and walked to the side of the yard. She picked up a thick iron pipe and went running for Big Man. Big Man had only taken his eyes off her for a few seconds, but it was a few seconds too long. Aunt Rosa was on him before he could get out of her path. She screamed a long, blood curdling cry and hit Big Man on his upper arm with all her strength. He was so tall that was as high as she could reach. He went down to one knee. She swung at his head with another death call and with all the power she could summon. The blow connected. Big Man's head squirted a spray of blood, the droplets showering Aunt Rosa's face as he keeled over onto the ground.

Transfixed by the scene, Carl was frozen in place. Jenney began to open her car door. Aunt Rosa was raising the pipe for another blow to Big Man's head. Carl followed Jenney from the car and ran to Aunt Rosa, grabbing her descending arm. Aunt Rosa struggled in his grasp and shouted her rage at his interference. Carl did not release his grip on Aunt Rosa, knowing he would be next if he dared let her go. Jenney began talking to her trying to calm her down. Big Man was now stirring, blood oozing and spurting from various open wounds. Aunt Rosa saw him struggling to stand. He managed to hold himself up on one knew. His face was streaked with blood still dripping from the side of his head. The blood had spread from one side of his neck to the other, painting him in a reddish hue. Aunt Rosa seemed to recover her senses, and broke free of Carl 's grip. She ran to Big Man and grabbed his face in both her hands. One hand on either side of his face, she began kissing him and crying and telling him she was sorry. She surveyed his wounds as if they had been invisible to her before. Big Man hugged her back. She howled, seemingly in pain.

Carl and Jenney got Big Man into the car, their plans to go home now amended. Big Man would need immediate medical care, so they were going to take him to the hospital. Aunt Rosa limped over to the car and Jenney let the window down. She was holding her right upper arm and said, "I broke my arm when I hit him with that pipe." She was still trying to tell Big Man how sorry she was for nearly killing him. Jenney tried to get Aunt Rosa to get into the car for the drive to the hospital, but she refused to go. She said she just wanted us to save Big Man's life, so she told Carl to go. He did.

Carl reached the hospital twenty minutes later and struggled to help Big Man out of the car. Ava's last impression was of the hospital staff trying to get the big man onto a gurney and finally letting him walk inside. Ava never saw or heard from him again.

CHAPTER 11

EVICTED

The week after school began again that year, Jenney and Carl were inside the house enjoying a lazy Saturday. Ava and Elena were playing hopscotch with neighborhood kids right next to Jefferey's huge yard. Ava had not wanted to play, but Lynette had not taken no for an answer. Jefferey was a Junior who lived with his father. His uncle Billy lived at the end of the long dirt road. Jefferey Sr. was mean, his skin was the darkest shade of black Ava had ever seen. Billy's seemed even darker. Billy's afro was so huge it made a big halo around his head. Billy was Lynette's dad.

The kids began to argue, and a shoving match ensued. Ava gave Billy's daughter Lynette a bloody nose and she ran home to tell. As the game continued, Ava soon noticed Billy stomping up the road. He was mad. He was pulling Lynette by the arm, nearly dragging her. He stopped right in front of Ava. He began yelling in her face, telling her to keep her hands off his daughter. He shoved Ava to the ground. Elena ran across the road and got Carl. Carl came out and all hell broke loose. The two men began shouting and cursing each other and the kids stood there wide-eyed. Billy. reached for his pistol and pointed it up into the air. He squeezed the trigger. The loud pop made the girls jump. Carl walked quickly back across the road, cursing the whole way to the house. He went up the steps faster than Ava had ever seen him move. Guessing what was about to happen, Ava grabbed Elena and led her back across the dirt road and into their own yard. They moved behind one of the cars. They peeked out to watch what would happen next.

Carl came back out with his 12- gauge shot gun and hid behind a tree. Billy hid behind another big tree in Jeffery's yard. The men exchanged insults, cursing each other from across the road. Billy took aim and fired a shot towards Carl, and he ducked behind his tree. The shot had missed. Carl waited a beat and then angled the shot gun. As soon as Billy peeked around the tree, Carl fired a shot. The shot gun blast sounded like a cannon and the little girls yelped and covered their ears. Tree bark exploded into the air along with pieces of Billy's Afro. Ava saw Billy drop his pistol and take off running back towards the road. Carl fired the shot gun again and Billy ran faster, leaving his daughter behind.

The following Monday the family received an eviction notice. Billy's wife worked for the landlord, and it was rumored they were having an affair. The landlord owned the mill where Carl worked, so he also lost his job. He had worked at the mill for over eight years and had no idea what to do next. With nowhere to go, Carl and Jenney packed the car with their things. They crammed the girls into the car and drove the hour's trek to Grandma Nancy's house.

Ava felt deeply sad and ashamed. She had caused all of this. If she had not hit Lynette, they would not have to move out. She had lost her temper over a stupid game, and it cost them their only place to call home. Now her dad was out of work and the family had nowhere to go. She did not want to leave the only home she had ever known, and she did not want to go to Grandma Nancy's house. She was not afraid, but she did not want to live near Jimmy.

Grandma Nancy was Jenney's mom, the one who had raised Jimmy. She was a powerhouse, working two jobs, raising the growing number of grandkids her other two daughters kept producing. She was pretty with long, black hair that draped down her back. Her skin tone was light, almost yellow and she had an easy smile.

Aunt Susan was divorced from her husband and had five kids. Aunt Ella was still married but had come back home with her four kids, leaving her husband behind in Georgia with his family. Grandma's house was crowded with all those kids living there. It was no surprise she and Paw-Paw Frank would not let Jenney and her family come in. Grandma would let them come into the house to wash up and eat during the day, but they were forbidden to come inside the house at night.

It was late August and the weather had begun to change. Temperatures were hot during the day but dipped to the low sixties on some nights. The family slept in the car in Grandma's front yard, huddling together for warmth. Mama did her best to keep them warm. She covered them with thick blankets on the cooler nights, but some nights were just too hot. They slept with the windows of the car rolled down on those hot, balmy nights, sweating as they fell into fitful sleep. The four were crammed into the car, still filled with items from the house they left behind. Ava and Elena were afraid they would have to live in the car forever.

One night, Grandma Nancy came to the window of the car with her grandkids sleeping inside. The night was cold and rainy. There was a storm coming, as she could tell by the lightning off to the east. She told Carl and Jenney to grab some blankets and get the kids inside. They slept on a pull-out couch in the living room of Grandma's house for the next six months.

CHAPTER 12
ABANDONED

In January of 1984, Carl got hired for work that took him out of the state for weeks at a time. He would come home every other week bringing money and gifts for the girls. During one of his work trips Jenney disappeared one day. Ava and Elena waited all afternoon. Evening came, and she had not yet returned. The girls had school the next day, so Grandma Nancy made them get hot baths and go to bed. Ava could not sleep. She sat up on the pull-out couch bed trying to read, but she was just waiting for her mother. She could not concentrate on the words on the page. There was a growing ache in her belly, not entirely unfamiliar. She finally fell asleep just after midnight. Her sleep was restless, plagued by familiar nightmares. Monsters chased her through wooded places, but she could not seem to run away or scream. She awoke feeling tired and her stomach hurt. Still early, she got herself and Elena ready for school. Mama had not come home.

Days passed. Then weeks. The family heard nothing from Jenney. Their dad was away at work. He had stopped coming home every weekend and the girls were lucky to see him once a month. He still managed to send money to Grandma for caring for his daughters. She used the money for household expenses, but never for the girls. They needed school clothes and decent shoes. The kids at school made fun of them because they often had to share.

Ava would stare out the window at night, looking for signs of Jenney driving up the road. She never spotted her. She was missing for almost a month when Carl finally came back. Ava overheard him talking to Aunt Susan, saying he had found her living with her cousin in Mobile. Carl said Jenney was an alcoholic and had started using drugs. She was out of her mind and did not plan to come back home. Ava began crying herself to sleep night after night. Her stomach seemed to hurt all the time.

Ava did her best to take care of her little sister. She would comb her hair the night before school and make sure she had a good bath. She made sure she sat close to her on the school bus because the other kids were always mean to them. They laughed at their clothes and made fun of their busted-out shoes. The kids said Ava talked like a white person and they picked on her for that. The other kids did not like that the two sisters made good grades, so they were ridiculed for that, too. Despite the bullying, the girls were pretty and smart. They had long, thick hair which Ava kept in neat ponytails. Both girls were always polite and soft spoken.

Ava began to lose focus. She barely paid attention in class. She no longer cared about her grades. She began daydreaming during her classes and kept forgetting to do her homework. She tried to avoid going to recess, preferring to stay in the classroom with her head down on her desk. Ava sometimes had the eighty-five cents she needed to buy a bag of chips and a juice, but she tried to wait until the other kids were outside before going to the concession stand. One day she found herself too late to buy a snack. She suddenly looked around the hallway and realized she was alone.

She could not remember where she was and where she was supposed to be. Her head felt funny and her thoughts were all out of place. Ava became confused. She went to the girl's bathroom on the other side of the building. She went to the stall on the end and locked the door. She sat there for long moments, until some girls started coming in. Not knowing where to go, Ava walked slowly down the long hall. There were doors on either side of the hall, but Ava had no idea which one was hers. She simply could not remember. It was if she had completely forgotten who she was. Ava opened the door of a classroom. The teacher was speaking to the crowded group and Ava took the first seat she could find. She could not remember seeing the teacher at school before. Her mind was still fuzzy, and Ava was getting more confused by the moment. She put her head down on the desk, trying to disappear. The teacher walked over. He told her she was in the wrong room and this was not her class. He asked her where she was supposed to be. Ava tried to whisper that she did not know, but the kids heard anyway. She looked around as they began whispering to each other and looking over at her. Ava got up and walked to the door. As she reached for the doorknob, she glanced over her shoulder at the kids behind her. She left to the sound of their collective laughter echoing after her, chasing her down the empty hallway.

Ava could not remember how she got there, but she was on the bus with her sister Elena later that evening. She was happy to go home, but there was nothing to quell the feeling of uncertainty she lived with each day. She was terrified of what was happening to her. Ava did not know what could have caused her to lose a whole day of time. She was afraid she was losing her mind. She decided then and there that she was not going to tell anyone. She was much too embarrassed. Ava went home and pretended the blank moments had never happened. They had enough to worry about already. With no friends and no one she felt she could talk to; Ava kept her growing list of problems to herself. Ava knew it would do her and Elena no good if people knew. People would judge and laugh at them even more. Besides, what could anyone do even if she told them she could not remember things sometimes? She would just have to find a way to deal with it all, just like she always had, on her own.

Ava and Elena went through their days going to school and doing chores. The girls missed having a mom and had no idea when their dad would show up to see them again.

One late Saturday morning in March, Ava saw her father, Carl walking into the yard. She yelled to Elena that Carl was here and each of them ran out to meet him. Carl did not give them hugs or kisses. Carl would never do that. Instead he bent to give them high five and walked with them to the country store a half mile away. Ava and Elena were so happy. Each girl grabbed one of their father's hands as they walked up the street. As they approached the store, Carl gave each girl a twenty-dollar bill. They bought candy and chips and sodas. When they got back to Grandma Nancy's house, Carl gave Elena another twenty. Seeing this, Ava held out her hand for hers. Carl slapped her a low five and told her that was all he had. He left shortly after that. It would be months before the girls saw either of their parents again.

CHAPTER 13
TEACHERS

Back at school the following year, 1985, Ava started skipping some of her classes. She found several empty rooms in the old building where no one ever went. She found a classroom in the corner of the u-shaped building. She began hiding out there until she heard the bell to go to Mrs. Taylor's class. Mrs. Taylor taught literature and she seemed to love her job. She would finish her lessons for the class early each day and tell them to turn off the lights. The kids who were interested would gather on the floor between the rows of books Mrs. Taylor had stacked on the surrounding shelves. She had placed a thick rug on the floor. The kids would lay there expectantly as Mrs. Taylor settled into her chair. She would face the kids and continue to read from their story of the week. Each week she began a new title. Ava was enthralled with each one. Mrs. Taylor read to them classic titles like The Red Badge of Courage, Of Mice and Men, and poetry from Chaucer and Shakespeare. She would ask questions of the kids after reading long passages, to make sure they understood. Ava began to look forward to Mrs. Taylor's readings more than anything else in her life. She wished she could sit and listen to the stories all day.

One day that April, after the class ended Mrs. Taylor pulled Ava aside. She asked her if she liked the stories and Ava told her she loved them and could not wait to see what would happen next with Henry. Mrs. Taylor gave a small, high laugh and patted Ava on the back. She gave her a paperback copy of The Red Badge of Courage and told her she could take it home. Ava was silent. No one had ever given her anything before. Mrs. Taylor smiled. She asked if Ava was alright. Ava nodded yes. Mrs. Taylor told her that when she was a little girl someone had given her a book. She said that ever since then, she could not stop reading and writing. She told Ava to get a notebook and start taking notes of things she read that she liked or hated. She said Ava would learn why soon. Ava asked her if that was homework, but Mrs. Taylor said "no, just write Ava. Read everything you can get your hands on. And write. You will learn why later."

Ava thought Mrs. Taylor was out of her mind, but she decided to give it a try. What else did a bored 11-year-old have to do? She spent her .35 cents meant to buy snack and bought an 80-page notebook instead. That night, Ava began taking notes from the book she was reading. Later, she began writing down her thoughts. She added times and places for her classes to the front cover, a schedule just in case she forgot again. She wrote down classroom numbers, teacher names and subjects. She would pull it out at the end of each class just to make sure she went to the right room. It became a source of comfort just knowing it was always with her.

By the end of month Ava had begun writing poems of her own. They were crude but she continued to try. Eventually, she felt more comfortable holding the pen. Her writing began to take on a new meaning for her, giving her a sense of power, she had never felt She could create. Any world she could imagine, she had the power to create. She could pour all her pain into a story or a poem. If she chose, she could get her thoughts out of her head and onto paper, just to express herself. Ava was overwhelmed with the possibility of it all as she realized; Mrs. Taylor had helped her find her outlet.

CHAPTER 14
SCHOOL DAYS

Ava and Elena were learning a new way of life. They played with their cousins, spending entire days outside on the weekends. Each morning they all got up, leaving the youngest ones behind, and trekked through the woods behind the house. There was an overgrown path, past Paw-paw's pig pens that led to a creek hidden deep in the woods. Ava and her cousins would catch crawfish in little traps they had made from chicken wire or else with their bare hands. They would walk barefoot in the creek, over the rocks digging their toes in the mud below. The six kids would walk the length of the creek until it was near dark and time to make their way back home. Easy days of running, jumping and enjoying being kids were the best times Ava ever had.

Things were quite different at school. Ava did not feel safe. She was constantly subjected to the ridicule of the other kids. One day Ava decided she would try to talk to one group of girls standing next to the swings. They were on the school playground. She heard music coming from a little radio one girl was holding. She did not know the song, but the girls were singing the lyrics to *When Doves Cry by Prince*. Her hands were shaking, and her palms began to sweat. Ava knew she had to decide. She could not continue to stand there, she would either have to go up to them and speak or walk away now. She made her decision. She was tired of being left out of everything and she wanted to change it. No one was ever going to speak to her if she did not speak to them first. She walked over to the group of girls and whispered a shy hello. They all turned to look at her. One of them snorted in laughter as they looked her up and down. Another girl whispered something to her friend. Ava was wearing a yellow dress her grandma had gotten from a bag of clothes donated to them. The other girls were all wearing jeans and nice shoes. Ava looked down at her feet. One of the girls turned and walked away, pulling a friend along. The rest followed. Ava got the message, so she did not go after them. She turned and looked around. All the kids were either playing with others or standing around talking in groups. She was the only one standing alone. Ava felt isolated. She felt her eyes well with tears, but she refused to let them fall. She walked slowly over to the chain link fence. There was a large mound of soil hardened by the protruding roots of a nearby tree. She lowered herself to the ground. She was careful to let her knees fall together to one side. As she sat alone, a tall, dark boy came over to her. He began to speak to her. Ava stayed quiet. The boy looked like he was much older than her, so Ava wondered why he was there. Most of the kids at recess were in her class or of a similar age. This boy was at least fourteen.

Ava stood from her perch on the ground and started to leave. The boy grabbed her ponytail. Ava winced and grabbed for his hand, but he yanked her to the ground. The boy began kicking Ava, laughing all the while. Ava tried to cover her face as she lay there and accepted the blows. There were no teachers around, no one came to help. The boy kicked her several more times and landed one last blow to her ankle. Finally satisfied he began to walk away. Ava struggled to get to her feet. As she took a step, the boy rounded on her and spit in her face. Ava began to limp away, holding her stomach. Her body felt the pain. She could hear him behind her, calling out in a taunting voice. "Come on, little girl don't run away. I have so much love to give you. Don't you want to see?" Ava made it into the hallway hoping to run into Mrs. Taylor. The boy was still coming behind. He was walking slowly, going in a zigzag, crossing from one side of the hall to the other. Ava tried to run. The boy was faster. He pushed her down to the floor. Ava scrambled back to her feet and tried to run again. The door to the classroom where Mrs. Taylor taught was open, so Ava dashed inside. The lights were off, and she could immediately see that she had made a big mistake. The room was completely empty. She turned to go out of the door, but the boy had already seen. He blocked her exit and pushed out his chest, getting closer to Ava, until she began to back further inside. Ava screamed and with a sudden burst of energy, tore a path towards the boy. She caught him off guard just enough to make him lose his balance. She did not stop. She ran around and past him and took the few steps to the classroom door. She ran down the hall blindly, with no destination in mind. As she ran, she noticed several teachers come out of their classrooms to see what the noise was about. One of them told her to stop running, but Ava never paused long enough to see the reaction as she turned the corner. She ran down the long hall and into the bathroom, cowering in the last stall.

Ava lost track of time. Her mind was completely blank. She did not know how, but she found herself on the school bus again later that day. It was like waking up, only to discover she had been sleepwalking. Her body was not in the last place she remembered. Ava could not explain.

Ava saw the boy several times after that, but she made sure he did not get near her. She avoided him at every opportunity. She began surveying her surroundings making sure he was not there. She was sure he would come for her again. He finally caught her off guard one day as she turned away from the water fountain. He smirked and reached for her hair. There were others in line to get water, but Ava did not notice. As he reached for her, she slapped him as hard as she could across the face. He never bothered her again after that. His name was Donnie.

CHAPTER 15
BONDING

Carl and Jenney were back together. They had gotten a small house for their family to live in. It was less than a mile down the road from Grandma's. Carl had gotten steady work driving trucks and things were starting to get better. One weekend, Carl came home with a white man in tow. He had picked him up on the side of the road trying to thumb a ride. The man was named Alton. Alton was tall, muscular and in his early forties. He wore his sandy blonde hair crew cut and had a fading scar over the right side of his upper lip. He had lost his wife and son, fallen on hard times and Ava's parents were helping him out.

Ava's mom and dad liked to go to the nearby nightclub and drink on Saturday nights. It was a hotspot for locals and out of towners alike. People would come from nearby Alabama and Mississippi towns to enjoy the infamous club. The club sat on a hill with a parking lot that filled quickly. The overflow of cars would line the narrow, paved road for half a mile on either side. Ava's parents would drink, party, and come home in the early morning. They always brought home cheeseburgers from the grill at the club and would wake their girls up to eat.

The family would take drives to visit other relatives quite often. Ava's favorite family drive was going to Mobile to visit her dad's sister, Maureen. Maureen was a little eccentric. She collected newspapers, cardboard, magazines, glass jars and everything else. Maureen could not seem to bear throwing anything away at all. In fact, it was getting increasingly harder to get inside her front door, because there was so much clutter. Aunt Maureen seemed to develop an emotional connection to every single piece she collected. She would become agitated if anyone attempted to remove or rearrange any of the items. Everyone soon learned to leave her growing pile of clutter alone.

Aunt Maureen had five kids with her husband Shane. The family whispered that Shane drank too much and got mean on the weekends. He would beat his wife and kids relentlessly whenever he had a bad day. He had caused one of the younger daughters to spend weeks in the hospital, recovering from several broken bones. Thankfully, Shane never came out of the bedroom when they drove down for a visit. Ava did not want to see him at all.

Ava particularly liked one of Aunt Maureen's sons, Shane Jr. He seemed kind and always showed Ava around his neighborhood. He took her on bike rides, loaning her one of his own. Even though he was six years older, he always took the time to make sure his cousins' visit was fun.

On a dreary day in mid-June 1985, Cousin Shane Jr. loaned Ava his bike. She had worn flip flops that day and they kept sliding off as they rode down the paved side street. They were about to turn around and ride the bikes back home when Ava's shoe slipped off again. Her foot snagged on the jagged bike pedal. As her foot caught, the skin ripped and tore, leaving blood and a chunk of meat behind. Ava fell off the bike and Shane Jr. came to her side. He carried her all the way back to his house on his handlebars. Ava was hurt, but she thought

Shane Jr. was cool for helping her get back to the house. He got peroxide and cleaned her cut, bandaging her foot himself.

A month later, Carl came home for the weekend. He brought Shane Jr. with him. Shane Jr. was in trouble with police and could not return to his home. Apparently, his father Shane Sr. had gotten drunk and beaten Shane's sister severely. Shane Jr. intervened and tried to stop his father from killing his sister. A vicious fight broke out in their home and Shane Jr. picked up a shot gun. He shot his father, killing him. Shane Sr.'s family vowed revenge, police were looking to arrest Shane Jr., so Aunt Maureen wanted him out of town. Carl agreed to let Shane Jr. stay with his family.

CHAPTER 16
A PREYING FAMILY

The following year, Ava was twelve and babysitting at home for her older cousin, Lisa. Lisa had no children of her own but was responsible for her younger brother and sister. Lisa and Ava's moms were first cousins who did not always get along. Despite the animosity, Ava's dad often took them to visit at Lisa's house. Lisa had asked Ava to babysit so that she could go out for the evening. One of the girls liked to play with Elena, so they would keep each other entertained. When Carl was ready to leave, Ava packed the kids and their things in the car. Lisa would come and get them Sunday morning before church.

Later that evening, Carl and Jenney decided to go out to the nightclub. Alton was in his room near the front door. Jenney took her time getting dressed in her close-fitting jeans. Carl had washed the car earlier in the day. The couple left the house around nine o'clock. Ava and the kids were scattered across the living room floor with blankets and pillows, bedded down for the night. Shane Jr. was lying on the couch. All the kids had fallen asleep, along with Ava and Elena.

Ava awakened with Shane Jr.'s finger inside of her. He was

stabbing in and out of her and telling her to be quiet. He pulled up her shirt and put his foul-smelling mouth on her breast. Ava whimpered, fearful and in pain. Shane Jr. put his hand over Ava's mouth and bit down on her tiny, undeveloped breast. Ava screamed, but it was muffled by Shane Jr's hand covering her mouth. One of the children stirred and Shane Jr. went still for a moment. When the child settled, Shane put his finger back inside her and began stabbing her mercilessly. His nails cut her, scraped her inside and out. She felt like he was ripping her apart. Shane grabbed Ava's throat and squeezed. His meaty hands were three times the size of hers as he pressed her into the floor. Shane ripped Ava's pajamas off and her underwear along with it. He straddled her, his penis already erect and protruding from his loose boxers. He spread Ava's legs, lifted her up and slammed himself inside of her. He pumped and grunted, raping her brutally, all the while covering her mouth with his hand. Each painful thrust made Ava grunt as tears flowed like a river down her face. "Ava?" called Alton from the room just down the hall. He had heard the noise and Ava heard him get out of bed. Her eyes darted from Shane's face to the direction of Alton's room. She could hear him hovering on the other side of the door. Shane covered her mouth and whispered harshly, "tell him you're ok or I swear I will kill you right here, right now!" Looking into his eyes, Ava could see that her cousin was insane. His pupils were dilated so that his eyes appeared all black. The pretty, kind, brown eyes she was used to seeing had disappeared. In confusion and alarm, Ava opened her mouth to scream, but Shane ground his fingers into her neck. He squeezed her so hard she could no longer breathe at all. A burning heat began to spread from her chest, over her neck and crept up into her face. His elbow was positioned down the center of her chest between her breasts. His weight was crushing her. She was gasping for air. Shane spoke again in a harsh, threatening whisper, "when I finish with you, your little sister is next if you don't shut up. I'll kill your mama and Carl, just like I killed my daddy." Ava was fighting just to breathe, but she nodded in compliance. She did not want her parents killed and she had to protect Elena. Shane released his grip on her throat, but he did not take his penis from inside her. Ava called to Alton to tell him she was alright. She knew her voice sounded weak and shaky, hoarse from Shane's hand squeezing her throat. Fresh hot tears ran down her face. She was filled with shame, rage, and overcome by fear. As Shane took what he wanted, she felt the remaining shreds of her innocence fade away. Ava Jackson died a little in that moment. She lay there, unmoving, accepting the assault of his lips, his brutal hands, and the pounding of his body on hers. He was crushing her, but he did not stop. Her body began to shake uncontrollably. Alton shouted from his room, "I'm coming in there." Ava knew he had an idea of what was happening to her at that moment. Shane did not finish. He moved off her but before he would stop his assault, he shoved his fingers inside of her little opening, forcing them as far as they would go. Ava felt him grab on to something inside of her and give a hard pull. Ava lost consciousness.

The next morning swollen and sore, Ava woke up in the worst pain she had ever felt. Someone had carried her to her bed, she suspected it was Alton. There was a bottle of pain killers and a glass of water by her bed, and she did not hesitate to gulp them down. She slept throughout the day, barely noticing the sounds in the house during the brief moments she was awake. As she slept, she dreamed feverishly. The monster was chasing her again. She felt his breath on the back of her neck and knew that he was closing in. This time she looked back. The monster wore a man's face this time. It was her cousin Shane. Ava awakened with a start. She was still alone in her room. She knew she had gotten up to use the bathroom, because her body was burning down there. Her insides felt torn to shreds. Her thighs were sore, and there was a bloody print of Shane's teeth on her breast. She knew everyone must have been out of the house because it was all quiet. She ran herself a warm bath and eased down into the water. The sting of the water touching her body made her breath catch in her chest and the hot tears began to flow once again.

CHAPTER 17
BETRAYED

Three days went by before Ava came out of her room. She had been waiting until the family went to bed at night before she would come out to get something to eat. She only dared small meals because her throat was too sore to swallow most solids. Luckily, Mama kept cans of soup in the kitchen which she heated as quietly as she could. She had not heard or seen Alton since the awful attack, but she did not know how she felt about that. She believed he had tried to save her, but he had not tried hard enough.

Shane had hurt her very badly. He had taken more than just her dignity and her body. He had broken her faith in family. She felt as though he had ripped open her soul. She had made the mistake of thinking he was her friend as much as they shared the same blood. Now she knew she had made a terrible mistake by allowing herself to trust him. She should have known better. She had believed she was safer with him around, instead he turned out to be the worst monster yet. She would never allow herself to be in the same room with him again, and she would never let him near her sister, Elena.

By the end of September, Shane was not living in their

house anymore even though no one knew what had happened. He was spending most nights with Aunt Susan and coming back to the house periodically.

Ava had withdrawn into her own corner of herself, not communicating with anyone at all. She would stay in her room and read books after school and refuse to come out. She would tell Carl her stomach hurt so she would be allowed to stay home on Sundays. She could not bring herself to go to church. God had abandoned her long ago. Her parents just had not realized that yet.

The fun-loving child was gone forever if she had ever been that. She had so many terrible secrets inside of her now and she knew she could not tell. Shane had said he would kill her mom and dad and hurt Elena too. She could not allow that to happen. The things she had endured before the move were also better left unspoken. She believed her mother knew some things anyway and had chosen to ignore them. Carl had no idea anything bad had happened at all. He was either working or just too busy living his life to notice what happened to her. Besides, if he had any idea, she was sure he would hunt them all down and kill them one by one. A part of her smiled at that thought.

Alton had left the morning after she was raped, and she had not heard anyone say where he had gone. She wished he had at least shown his face so that she could ask him a few questions. She would like to know what he heard and if he knew what Shane was doing at the time. She wanted to ask why he did not stop him. She wanted to say goodbye. She guessed it was just as well.

Ava's nightmares returned that week. She would find herself trying to run but her legs did not seem to move at all. She turned to look behind her knowing the monster was catching up to her. In her dreams she would scream, but no sound came from her mouth. Her monster now had a face. Ava would awaken drenched in sweat, chest heaving from her racing heart.

The next week Mama and Aunt Susan took Ava and a few of the smaller kids for a drive to the store in town. The two adults chatted in the front seat as Ava read her book, ignoring the kids in the backseat with her. When they returned home, Aunt Susan stopped the car in front of Mama's house. As she was cutting the engine, Ava opened her door to step out. Aunt Susan said "no, you stay. We have something to tell your mama." Ava was puzzled. She had not seen or spoken to her aunt in weeks. What could "they" possibly have to discuss?

Aunt Susan began telling Mama that Ava was not what she seemed. She said Shane had told her that Ava had tried to seduce him. Ava gasped and nearly choked. Aunt Susan said Shane had told her that Ava was a hot little firecracker and had tried to get him to have sex with her. Ava felt that old rage boiling up from somewhere deep inside. She could not take these lies anymore and she finally found her voice. She told them exactly what Shane had done to her and just how badly he had hurt her. Mama was crying by the time Ava finished, but she was mad at Ava for not telling her sooner. Ava said, "Mama you don't know anything about what has happened to me my whole life!!" Aunt Susan held her gaze in the mirror, her eyes suspicious, accusing, and filled with unmistakable hatred. Ava screamed at them both to just leave her alone. She opened the door furiously and ran back inside the house and locked herself in her room.

Later that evening, Carl burst into her room, breaking the door from the hinge. He was yelling at Ava, calling her a whore. He had his thick leather belt and began beating her relentlessly. He hit her all over her legs, thighs, back, arms and face. Ava felt each blow rip off another layer of her soul, as her skin opened in several places. She was screaming and trying to shield herself, to no avail. Carl ignored her screams and beat her until he was spent.

By Thanksgiving, the bruises had faded, and Ava simply felt hollow inside. She found pleasure in nothing at all. She had no friends at school, and her grades had started to slip once again. She was glad for the holiday break because she just did not have any interest in anything her teachers had to say. Most days she spent her time at school daydreaming or staring at nothing. She had taken to biting her nails which were usually healthy and long.

Ava was angry with Aunt Susan. She felt that she had violated her all over again. Aunt Susan took Shane's side and did not believe Ava. Ava did not understand how she could humiliate her that way. She could still feel the hot shame flush her face when Aunt Susan's accusatory gaze held hers in the rearview mirror. She could not figure out why her aunt seemed to hate her so much that she deliberately caused her more pain. Ava felt betrayed by her family. She would never trust any of them again.

CHAPTER 18
THANKSGIVING DINNER

Thanksgiving was different than in previous years. Ava's mom cooked at home and some family came over to eat. Ava helped her mom in the kitchen, as she had done every year. She cut up the bell peppers, onions and celery and sautéed them for their dressing. She helped cook the large pot of black-eyed peas and she made the potato salad all on her own. She felt good about her efforts. Mama baked a few pies and a chocolate cake.

The table was heavy with so many dishes and everyone grabbed a plate. Carl had invited Aunt Maureen and her daughters and Ava thought that was strange. She could not figure out how they would react to her after what happened with her son Shane. Everyone piled their plates high with food. They sat down on the couches and chairs in the small living room. Carl blessed the food. When everyone raised their heads at the end of the prayer, Carl raised his voice once more. He told everyone to wait just a moment he had one more thing to say. He looked at Ava and said, "now you tell them what he did!" Ava's mouth dropped open. She looked around at all the faces staring back at her and was not sure she had heard correctly. She asked her father to repeat his words. He said it once more only this time he commanded her to stand in the center of the room. He instructed her to tell exactly what had happened, leaving out no details. Tears welled in Ava's eyes as humiliation made her cheeks burn. She stood there, mute for a moment, until Carl began to take off his belt. Ava started speaking. She sobbed as she told of her shame. She kept her eyes on the floor in front of her feet and repeated the story of the brutal rape. She could feel their eyes burning into her skin, some doubtful and others sad. She wanted none of their judgmental opinions and abhorred their pity for her. Ava was strong in her conviction; she was not the one who had done wrong. Still, shame coursed through her in waves.

When she was finished, she turned and walked into her room. Ava was torn apart. She could not understand how God could abandon her to so many horrors. She did not want to fight anymore; she had no reasons left. Ava wondered why she was here in this cold, cruel world. Why was she ever born? She did not eat Thanksgiving dinner.

That was the first time Ava began to contemplate ending her life. She felt worthless and without hope. Her family was separate and apart from her. She did not feel she belonged. No one seemed to believe her even though she told the truth. Ava had not lied to them about anything. Somehow, they were still blaming her for being raped. Ava felt that she had now been raped by all of them, Shane, her father, and Aunt Susan. How could she ever tell any of the other things she had endured? No one would bother to listen. They would probably say she made it all up, just like they were saying now. Her father would beat her senseless. Ava knew that she could not trust anyone with the secrets of her past. She stored them all in a tiny corner of her mind. She thought it was better to pretend they were not there. Somehow, the pile of bad memories just seemed to continue to grow. No matter how good she tried to be as a person, she kept getting hurt. Ava was lost and uncertain, with nowhere at all to turn.

Ava began to have stomach pains in earnest. She could not go to school. Fear seemed to rule her every waking moment and overcome her when she slept. Jenney would call her to get dressed for school and Ava would start to complain. She ended up staying in bed on those days reading and eating soup. Ava missed fifty-three days of school that year alone. The school noted it on her report card for the end of the year, but they passed her on to the next grade. Her grades had slipped, but not enough to affect her final average.

CHAPTER 19
COMING OF AGE

Ava was not like most girls her age. At fourteen, she did not talk about boys, had no interest in parties or school dances, and had given up trying to make friends. Ava was petite, skinny and her creamy dark skin seemed to be more of a deterrent than a magnet for the boys she knew anyway. Boys called her mean names and made jokes about her small size. The girls avoided her altogether. She was never invited to any of their parties or sleep overs. Sometimes she overheard them whispering about her, calling her ugly and saying she had no class.

Ava did not care what they thought of her. She spent all her time daydreaming of a life without pain. She had long since given up her childish ideas of being rescued by some nice family who did not allow their children to suffer. She knew no one was going to save her. Ever. She only talked to the pen pals she wrote to and her only friend Daniel Beck. Danny's father, Billy went to church with them and often visited their home. Sometimes, Ava and Elena stayed at Billy's house between church services and would rejoin their parents at the second service. Danny had come to live with his father after years in

New York and he and Ava became fast friends. Danny was older than Ava, white but she knew that did not matter. The few people she spoke to on occasion at school were white too. In fact, none of the black people in her school accepted her. Her days at school were spent trying to ignore their constant barrage of insults and ridicule.

Danny was the first person she felt understood her experiences, as she learned he had many of his own. He seemed to have a brooding energy about him which matched her need for solitude. Danny and Ava often shared books and a love of writing poetry. It became a source of mutual comfort to exchange their written creations. They would sometimes sit together in her room for hours, both buried in their own novel or original works, without speaking a word. Sometimes they listened to some music. Ava had a collection of albums and 45's. She and Danny listened to Keith Sweat, Billy Ocean, Terence Trent D'Arby, and George Michael. They loved Bobby Brown and Freddie Jackson. Danny gave her music from Salt 'n Pepa and The Jets. Ava developed a love for music that nearly matched her love for reading. She felt a strong connection with the emotions in the songs. Music provided Ava a welcome release for her loneliness.

Ava spent most of her time alone in her room reading and writing poems. She had written so many, she had to buy a large binder to secure them all. She never shared her poems with anyone other than Danny, until a nice white couple from her church found her writing in her book one day. The nice lady, sister Millie posted one of her poems on the church bulletin board and told Ava she was quite talented. Ava felt a surge of pride but did not think too much on the subject.

Ava was distracted by other things. Her stomach pains had begun to take on a different feeling. She would become tired and have even less interest in the things going on around her. One day at school the pain became intense, so she went to the girl's bathroom. As she sat on the toilet, she felt that she could not stop urinating. She looked down and found that the toilet was filled with blood. Ava was terrified. What was wrong with her private parts? Did she hurt herself or get cut somehow? Ava did not know what to do. She stayed in the bathroom most of the school day thinking she had somehow offended God. The blood was a punishment, sent to deepen her shame for her sins. Ava looked at the jeans she wore and found the blood had soaked through them. Ava was dismayed. Her clothes were hopelessly soiled, and everyone was going to see.

Eventually, she realized she had no choice but to put her clothing back on. She stuffed her bloody underwear into a wad of tissue and pushed it into the garbage can. She made a second wad and stuffed it between her legs. The blood kept coming. She pulled on her pants and left her shirt outside, hoping it draped low enough to cover the stains. She went to the office to use the phone and call her mom. She was so afraid she had done something to cause this mysterious bleeding, she did not tell her mom at first. When they got home, Ava finally asked her mom what was happening to her. Jenney explained that every female has a menstrual cycle and will bleed once a month. Ava was mortified. She said, "you mean it's going to happen again?" Jenney laughed at her daughter's incredulous expression. "Yes, every single month it will happen again." Ava's mom hugged her. She went to the store and got her some necessary items and told her to read the instructions. She made her some hot tea and gave her soup and crackers and told her to lie down. Ava did not return to school that week because of the intense pain. She missed 38 days of school that year.

CHAPTER 20
STALKED

Ava's parents had taken to letting her walk the nearly three miles to Grandma Nancy's on her own. Ava liked the long walk because she could think without people interrupting. One afternoon, she decided to visit Aunt Susan, who had built her house next door to Grandma's. Grandpa owned the land there, so this was a convenient choice. The two houses shared a big yard, so going from one to the other was an easy walk. Ava knocked on the door, which was open and heard her aunt say "come in." As Ava walked through the door, a movement down the hallway to her left caught her eye. Aunt Susan's new boyfriend stood in the doorway of their bedroom staring back. He dropped his robe to the floor and fondled his naked penis. Ava turned and walked out the door again.

Ava stopped going to Grandma's for a few months because she knew Uncle Perv, her nickname for Earl, would be waiting for her. This time she did not keep secrets. She told her mom and dad about Uncle Perv showing her his private parts. They went to tell Aunt Susan. Aunt Susan told Ava's parents it was all lies and that Ava was just seeking attention. She said Ava was not the innocent fourteen-year-old her parents thought her to be. Aunt Susan said Earl would never do such a thing. She said that Ava probably just imagined it because she wanted him to look at her that way.

One evening her parents left in the car to go to Grandma's house. Ava stayed home. The shrill ring of the telephone caught her off guard. Ava ran from her room and answered "hello." No one replied. "Hello," Ava said again. The caller hung up. Five minutes later, the phone rang again, and Ava slowly picked up the receiver. There was someone on the other end breathing heavily into the phone. The sound was disturbing and sexual and Ava thought she knew who it was. When her parents came home, she told them about the calls. Carl got the phone and reverse called the number. Uncle Perv answered the call. Carl slammed the phone down and walked quickly back to his car. He went to Aunt Susan's house and demanded to speak with Earl. Earl denied everything and Carl knew he was lying. He told him he would kill him if he called or came near Ava again.

Several weeks passed and no other incidents occurred. Ava began to relax again. One Saturday morning, her parents left for Grandma's house. Ava was sitting in her room listening to music. She had newly discovered Betty Wright and Denise LaSalle and managed to get cassette tapes of their recordings. She was intrigued by the lyrics. She thought she heard a scraping sound outside her bedroom window. She lowered the volume on the cassette player she was listening to. The sound came again, more pronounced this time and she moved closer to the window. She reached to open it so she could peer outside, but a big face appeared right in front of her. Uncle Perv was right outside. She panicked. Her parents would not come home for hours. She was here all alone. What if he tried to get in? She remembered the front door was unlocked and raced towards the front of the house. As she neared, she heard footsteps stomping onto the porch. Ava grabbed the doorknob and felt the tension that told her he was twisting it from outside. She struggled to turn the lock in the center. She pushed at the deadbolt, trying to slide it into place. She could feel the door trying to give way and open under Earl's tugging. She gave a sudden yank and felt the deadbolt slide into place just enough to keep it locked. Ava felt the pressure from the other side of the door ease just as she heard and felt a loud thud. Uncle Perv had banged his fist against the outside of the door in frustration. Ava got a sick feeling in the pit of her stomach. Everything had gone quiet. She saw movement out the window to her right. She was tearing down the hallway in an instant trying to beat him to the backdoor. She yelped in fear when she heard him pull on the door seconds before she got to it. She reached the door and snatched the handle, turning the lock as she slammed the door into place. She was sure she only managed to wrench it from his hands because he did not expect her to make it there in time to stop him.

Earl cursed loudly and beat on the back door. He made his way to the front and tried to get in again. Hoping the lock would hold, Ava grabbed the telephone and dialed her grandma's number. She frantically told Grandma Nancy what was happening and heard her yelling for Carl. She told them to get back to the house right now because Earl was trying to get Ava. Carl must have left in a flash because he was back in their yard within five minutes. Earl was long gone by then. Ava answered all his questions and Carl called the Sheriff. She later heard her parents talking amongst themselves. They said a restraining order was issued, and Earl was ordered to stay away from Ava.

Ava decided she had to stay away from that man. He was a monster just like all the others. He pretended to be nice and kind until no one else was around. Ava was frightened of him. She did not want to be caught alone with him on the loose.

What if he was angry with her for telling and came after her? Ava was sure he would try again. Even if the sheriff told him to stay away there was no guarantee. Ava began to have vivid nightmares of being chased again. She could see and hear the monsters getting closer than ever before. She felt lost and on her own. She would wake up covered in heavy perspiration, as though she had been running. Ava curtailed her walking, afraid she would be caught out on her own, defenseless. She felt like such a coward, but she knew it was not safe to go out on her own. She would have to wait until things settled down. She wished she never had to see Earl's face again.

Aunt Susan married him two years later.

CHAPTER 21
NEW BEGINNINGS

Ava and Elena got off the school bus in front of their house. It was the beginning of summer break and both girls were excited to be out of school. As they walked in the house, they immediately knew something was going on. Their parents were sitting in the living room waiting for them to arrive. Jenney seemed upset and Carl seemed like his usual ornery self, although Ava detected a current of excitement resonating within him as well.

As the girls settled, Carl told them rather bluntly that they were going to Mobile. Ava thought someone must be in the hospital because that was the only time they ever went there. Carl put an end to that early on, announcing they were going to visit their older sister. The girls exchanged glances. Ava, now 15 and Elena, newly aged 12 had never even heard of another sibling. How could their parents have had another kid they had never even mentioned? Carl said it was his child from a previous relationship, from before he had married Jenney, their mom.

The family of four drove to Mobile supposedly to meet their long-lost sister and returned home a family of six. The sister, Vanessa had just given birth to her first child, a three-month-old boy named Michael. Carl decided to take them in. The family house only had two bedrooms, so this meant the girls had to make room for Vanessa and her baby in theirs. Carl put a twin bed next to the full and the two new additions moved in.

Ava was angry. She had never dreamed her father had a grown kid out there somewhere, invisible all this time. She struggled to reconcile her place in the family. She had always believed she was the oldest child. She had no reason to ever suspect otherwise. She had cared for her little sister, making sure she was clean, fed, and presentable. She protected her at school and did all the things a big sister should do. What was her place now? Had she just been replaced? There were no answers to be found.

Vanessa Rutledge was in her early twenties and the spitting image of Carl. She was not pretty by any stretch of kindness. Vanessa was born in a small town in Alabama. Her mother was reportedly insane. Rumors were that she was an alcoholic who had been accused of brutally beating her children. She had beaten her children so badly that one of the younger girls ended up wearing a full body cast for months while her little bones healed. The local authorities were forced to commit Vanessa's mom to a mental hospital where she spent the next several years.

Vanessa was mentally sane, but angry at the world. She had a rough up-bringing and it had taken a toll on her for sure. Vanessa failed to form an emotional attachment to her baby, Michael. She told multiple stories about who his father was, so the family could never be sure. Vanessa would get upset when little Michael cried in the middle of the night and she refused to try to comfort him. Once, as she was giving the baby a bath, the whole family turned at the sound of his sudden scream of pain. Vanessa had pushed the bar of soap just inside his rectum. Vanessa said it was an accident, but her face betrayed her words. Ava gave Michael his baths after that.

Ava walked to Grandma Nancy's house, just to get away from home. The cute little baby sure screamed a lot and his mother would just ignore him. Ava often found herself holding the baby, singing him back to sleep. She would walk with him outside under the moonlight and stars until he was calm. Michael soon captivated Ava and Elena. Both girls doted on him. They could soon see how intelligent the baby boy was and began spending all their time with him.

CHAPTER 22
STATUTORY

At fifteen, Ava had no friends. She was still being bullied and teased by the other teenagers she went to school with. Her first day of ninth grade had been an education in and of itself. They were bussed from the middle school to the high school in Silas, Alabama. As they got off the school bus, the newbies were led through a long, covered walkway. The walkway ended at a double set of steps with a landing in between. There was a line of boys standing on both sides of the walkway all the way to the top. As the freshmen girls walked through, the boys began heckling, catcalling, and whistling. "Fresh meat, fresh meat," was the main chorus being lobbed at the girls as they walked. They were reaching out grabbing girls' boobs and smacking their behinds. Ava tried to keep her head low and rushed up the steps. Someone reached for her backside and Ava quickly ran the rest of the way up.

Each day seemed like another episode of torture she would have to endure. The girls at school had all developed breasts and their hips were starting to flare. Ava would look down at her bare chest and wonder what was wrong with her. She still preferred reading to boys, and she did not want to go to any of the local hang outs. The kids from school all hung out at each other's homes, so Ava would not have been invited anyway. Still, she thought it would be nice if just one thing about her body could appear normal.

When school was out for the summer that year, Jimmy came back to stay at Grandma Nancy's. He began bringing a new girl around to visit. Her name was Phyllis and she was tall and quite beautiful. She took an interest in Ava and invited her to come home with her to meet her family one weekend. Phyllis said she had sisters and cousins that Ava would like.

Carl was so strict with Ava; he would not let her go with Phyllis until he and Jenney had met the girl's family in person. Phyllis lived in Mississippi and the drive took almost an hour.

Carl and Jenney got along well with Phyllis' family and began visiting them a few weekends each month. Ava made fast friends with Nakia, Phyllis' seventeen-year-old niece. The adults would get together and play cards while Ava and Nakia talked about books and their future.

Ava had never considered what she wanted to become in life. She had never thought of her future her at all. Each day for her seemed a repeat of the day before, and Ava was just trying to survive. Nakia was different. She taught Ava that it was important to plan. Nakia knew she wanted to become a lawyer. Ava was amazed. She had never met another black girl who wanted to become a lawyer. In fact, the black girls she grew up around only talked about having babies and getting married. Ava did not know if she wanted anything out of life, but she knew she did not want that.

Nakia introduced Ava to the rest of her family, which turned out to be huge. There were uncles, aunts, first cousins, nieces, nephews, and friends all around. Ava liked Angie, Nakia's twenty-four-year-old cousin because she made everyone else laugh every time she came over. The family had various houses, but Nakia and her mom shared the nicest of them all. Their home was not wood, but brick with four bedrooms, a spacious living room and dining area and a large kitchen. Ava could see the entire house was immaculate, with everything skillfully placed.

Finally, Carl agreed to allow Ava to spend a weekend with Nakia. Ava was so excited to spend time with her friend, the first one she had ever made. She packed her bag in a hurry, choosing shorts and t-shirts since she knew they were not going to do any outings. Carl drove her there himself.

Ava and Nakia spent the day talking and going over Nakia's plans. They made brownies in the large family kitchen. They took her younger nephews outside and chased them around the yard, letting them play with the basketball. Exhausted and hungry, they all went to get washed up for dinner. Nakia's mom worked long hours, and Nakia was used to cooking dinner on her own. She let Ava help this time. They made macaroni and cheese, butter beans, fried chicken, and sweet tea. Nakia baked the cornbread. The family did not eat until Nakia's mom came home and washed up. Nakia and Ava set the table. The family held hands and gave thanks for the wonderful meal.

That night around nine, Angie came by all dressed up and ready to go out for the evening. She wanted to borrow a lipstick from Nakia. Angie asked if the two girls wanted to go with her. Nakia said no, but Ava jumped at the chance. She knew this would be the only chance she had to do something so grown up. Nakia did not seem to mind and told Ava to go and have fun. She helped Ava dress in an outfit she borrowed from Angie. Nakia did her hair. She made up Ava's face with just a bit of eyeliner and a touch of lip gloss. Ava was ready to leave.

Angie drove her little car to another house shrouded by trees. She did not pull her car close to the house, instead she turned off the lights and waited near the tree lined road. Moments later, Angie's cousin Kent got into his red Chevy

Beretta and reversed the length of the driveway. Angie said, "get out, you're riding with Kent and we will meet at the store down the street." Ava made the switch. Her heart beat a little faster sitting next to such a tall handsome guy. Kent was 6'4" and undeniably attractive. He had an easy smile and a quiet, observant demeanor. He put Ava at ease by asking her about herself. She told him her age and that she had never gone out with friends before. Kent said fifteen was a good age, but he was glad he was now nineteen. He said he was glad he was out of high school and enjoyed working and going to college.

They reached the store and stopped to pick up Angie. Ava got out of the car and moved to get into the back seat. Angie told her to stay up front and she climbed into the back instead. They drove down highway 84 in Mississippi which quickly became highway 45 in Alabama. Ava recognized this road and knew they were going to Mobile. Kent stopped just short and made a left onto a street in Citronelle. The street was small and narrow but there were cars lined up and down on both sides. They parked and got out and walked down the street, Ava in the rear. Angie was excited and raced ahead, leaving Ava far behind. Kent led her to the door of a run-down wooden structure. The door opened, and the sounds of pulse-pounding music assaulted Ava's ears. Ava began to get butterflies in the pit of her stomach as they neared the entrance. She saw that Kent paid money to the doorman sitting just inside. She tugged on his sleeve to let him know she had no money to pay and would need to go wait in the car. Kent laughed at her and said, "don't worry, I already paid for you." Ava smiled demurely and wrung her hands.

They entered the tiny shack of a building and stopped just inside. Kent walked away and came back with two cups of beer. He gave one to Ava and she began gulping it down. She could not tell if her palms were sweating or if the moisture was coming from the cup. Ava was on her second drink when she suddenly gasped and grabbed Kent's shirt. She moved to hide herself behind him and Kent asked her what was wrong. Ava could not believe her eyes. She had just seen Jimmy across the room talking to Vanessa. What were they doing here, of all places? Ava had thought she was safe from everything in her world. This was supposed to be her rare moment away from her entire family. Why were they here? Kent got Angie's attention and told her to go handle it. Angie went over to talk to Jimmy. She came back moments later and told Ava not to worry, her secret was safe, and her mom and dad would never know she was here. She looked at Jimmy and he gave her a thumbs up sign.

Ava relaxed after that and began enjoying the music. This was her first time coming to a place like this and there was so much to see. She began to take notice of the people, smoking, drinking, others making out, but everyone was having a good time. The party seemed to be in full swing, with no one ready to leave. Kent pulled Ava towards the door. Ava was not ready to leave yet, but she allowed him to lead her outside. He held onto her hand as he led the way back to his car. Ava felt lightheaded and she was sure there were butterflies running loose in her stomach. They walked around to the passenger side of the Beretta. He held the door for Ava to get inside before turning to walk around to slip into the driver's seat.

Kent reached for Ava's hand again and began to raise it to his lips. Ava felt her heart flutter. Kent grabbed the back of her head and lowered his mouth to hers. He kissed her gently, sweetly until Ava could no longer think. Ava had never felt like this. Her head was spinning, heart pounding thumping a steady beat. Kent reached across Ava's body and suddenly her seat was lying down. Kent moved on top of Ava and began kissing her again. He lifted her shirt and pushed her bra upwards. Ava stiffened. Things were moving much too fast. She barely even knew Kent at all. He began kissing her breasts, and Ava felt her breath coming in short, harsh, gasps. Her body had never felt such sensations. Kent raised himself off her body and pushed her pants to the floor. He lifted Ava while lowering his body onto hers. Kent looked into her eyes, questioningly. Ava felt he was asking her permission. She relaxed and lay back on the seat. Kent kissed her once more. Ava put her arms around his shoulders as he entered her. She closed her eyes tight and then heard a knock on the window above her. Kent moved away fast, but Vanessa had seen the two of them having sex in the front seat of his car. She was walking away quickly muttering loudly about telling their dad.

The night was over. Kent got Angie and took them back to get her car. Angie drove Ava to Nakia's house and dropped her off. Ava had barely fallen asleep when a car horn sounded outside. Carl was there to pick her up even though she was supposed to stay all day and go home later in the evening.

Ava was filled with dread, knowing Vanessa had ratted her out. As she had expected, Carl let loose on her as soon as she was in the car. Carl said he should never have trusted her, and she was never leaving the house again. Jenney sat quietly until later. She told her daughter she was turning out to be a grave disappointment. Ava cried tears of shame as Jenney shook her head. She endured the verbal assault the entire drive back home. Once there, Carl told her to go to her room and stay.

Ava was confused. Her feelings were all over the place. She was not sure how to react. She liked Kent a lot and she thought he liked her too. She had never done anything like that in her life. She had defied her parents and hurt them very badly. Still, she had never liked a boy before. Now, she would be forbidden from seeing him ever again. Her parents were mad enough to kill her, it seemed. She could remember the look of hurt and disappointment in her mother's eyes as she had come to the car this morning. Would they ever forgive her? Ava was not sure if she wanted them to forgive her as much as she wanted to talk to Kent.

Carl ordered Ava to the living room. Once there he made her sit down. He wanted her to tell him what happened. Ava recounted the events. She told her dad she wanted to see Kent again, an act of courage she had never dared before. Carl was livid, and the yelling and cursing began again. This time, Ava shouted back. Her parents kept saying Kent was too old for her, but she told them that was not true. "He's only four years older than me, how is nineteen too old?" Jenney said she had called and spoken with Nakia's mom, and she had told her something different. She said that Kent was 24, married and had two small children. His wife had learned about the incident and taken her kids back to her family's home. She was saying she wanted a divorce.

Ava was floored. How could any of this be the truth? Kent had said he was single and only nineteen. Ava could not believe it. She had to talk to Kent or Nakia and find out the truth for herself. Ava defied her father and took the phone into her room and dialed Nakia's number. Nakia confirmed that the story her parents told her was correct. She had been lied to.

Her father called the police to press charges on Kent for statutory rape. Ava refused to speak to them. She did not want him to go to jail. She could have told Kent to stop at any time, but she had not. Why should he be punished for that?

Kent had done nothing wrong. Ava had let him touch her because she liked the way he made her feel. He had been so kind and considerate. He had made her feel interesting and relevant for the first time ever. No one had ever spoken to her before, not like that. Now everything was ruined, and he would never speak to her again. Still, he should have told her the truth. Ava would never have let him kiss her if she had known he had a family. That was not cool at all. Maybe she was better of staying away from him after all.

CHAPTER 23
MISTAKES

Ava spent most of the summer lamenting her mistakes. She was still sad but coming to terms with the fact that she had made a bad decision. She felt an incredible guilt that a family was hurt by her choices. Even though she did not know about Kent's family until after that night, she was still partly to blame. She wished she could speak with the whole family and apologize for her part in the whole sordid mess. She knew she had hurt them all.

She had lost the only friend she had. She felt that with a deep sense of sadness and regret. She hoped Nakia would forgive her and that they would regain their friendship one day. She knew that was not likely.

Ava began a habit of walking down the street past the night club Carl and Jenney used to frequent. She walked farther and farther and began to visit her aunt Rosa. Aunt Rosa had bought a new house at the front end of a long dirt road. Ava was so bereft after losing her friend and her family's respect, she just enjoyed the solitude of the walk. Aunt Rosa welcomed her each day and made her lemonade. She would make her laugh despite Ava's sadness. She would read Ava's palm and tell her things about her future. Aunt Rosa said Ava would go to college because she had images of her in a classroom. She said she would get married and have a son. Ava thought Aunt Rosa was losing her mind, but she dared not say so aloud.

One day as she was leaving Aunt Rosa's a car pulled up and stopped next to her. There was a family inside and Ava knew them all. Miss Kelley lived on the other end of the dirt road and asked her if she wanted to come with them. She said they were having a family barbecue and Ava looked like she needed to eat. Miss Kelley would not take no for an answer, so she squeezed into the car. They drove over the muddy, red dirt road avoiding large potholes along the way. Ava waited outside for Miss Kelley and her daughter to finish the food. There were lots of people in her small yard preparing the grill, playing cards, and drinking beer.

Kelley's son came outside and sat on the wooden bench next to Ava. Ava remembered him from school. He used to harass her every day and Ava would run away. He had tried to kiss her once and she had slapped his face. Ava did not like this boy at all.

Donnie sat next to her and tried to start a conversation. Ava just listened. Donnie continued to talk, and Ava felt uncomfortable, so she got up and walked away. No one came after her and Ava made her way back home. Donnie began stopping by her house asking to speak to Ava. Ava started to mellow towards him after a few weeks and the two began to date. Carl did not seem to mind. Ava and Donnie began a sexual relationship that only lasted until the end of summer. When school began again in the fall, Donnie seemed to want an end to their relationship.

One evening on the bus ride home, Donnie was on the last seat in the back. Ava was sitting three seats in front of him. They had not spoken to each other since school began. Donnie was sitting next to his friend whom everyone called Pig. Pig began throwing orange peels and hitting Ava with them. Ava turned and calmly told him to stop. Pig threw another and Ava stood and turned around. She dared him to do it again. He did. Ava took her heavy textbook and sailed it towards Pig's head. It connected with a satisfying thud. Blood trickled onto his forehead where the book had made contact. Pig became enraged. He threw the book and Ava reached out and caught it before it could connect with her head. She was so incensed she climbed over the two seats between them and began pounding Pig's face. Donnie intervened and punched Ava, knocking her backwards into the seat. Ava still refused to give up. She climbed to her feet and punched Donnie right back. The two boys began pounding on Ava. Each of them was landing hard blows to her face, head, and stomach. Ava could see the fists coming and she knew they were connecting, but she did not feel any pain. The boys' blows forced her down on the seat, the other occupant long gone, trying to avoid the fight. Ava was trapped on her back and the two of them were beating her relentlessly. She felt the vestiges of helplessness begin to take over her mind. She remembered feeling this way when Shane held her down and she thought she was going to die. Suddenly Ava was no longer afraid. She felt her blood begin to boil and a rage seemed to take over her. She pulled both her legs into her chest and mentally gathered her strength. She kicked Donnie as hard as she could, and he fell back into the window. She got to her feet standing on the bus seat and she and Pig had a punching fest then. Ava was relentless. She felt her nails rake across his face tearing the skin as they went. Pig banged Ava's head into the bus window, so Ava grabbed his and did the same. She wrapped both hands around his throat and slammed his head again and again. The stronger boy punched every part of her that he could reach but Ava would not let him go. Finally, the driver stopped the bus and came to pull Ava away. Her face was bloody, and her lip was split open from the repeated blows. Ava did not feel any pain. Still in her rage, she laughed and taunted both boys about how it took two of them to get her down and they each looked worse off than she did. Donnie was still holding his chest where she had kicked him when they forced her back onto the seat. His top lip was already swelling, and the bottom was bleeding. Pig's nose was bleeding and he had deep gouges along his jaw.

Days later, Donnie began telling his friends about having sex with Ava over the summer. His pride must have been hurting because he started telling them she was easy and loose. Ava did not care what they thought. They had never been kind to her, so why should it matter now. She had endured years of bullying and verbal assault from all of them and one more insult would not make or break her will. She knew the truth about who she was. She was a survivor, and that was exactly what she would continue to do. Only now, she would not just lay down and accept their punishment. She would start to fight back.

CHAPTER 24
A TEENAGE LOVE

Ava was sixteen and still painfully shy. She always tried to avoid the other kids. She had learned that they were meaner when they were in groups. Ava tried to time her comings and goings in the hallway so that she would not see them, but that was not always possible. Each encounter seemed to have the potential to escalate if she engaged with them, so she usually just endured the verbal assault.

One morning a group of girls walked behind her as she was leaving her Consumer Math class. One was tall and the other was not. Both were pretty and loved to pick on Ava. Usually they called her ugly and said she was a waste of space. This time, the tall girl said, "look at how she walks, I think she's in a gang," and the other girl laughed loudly. Ava decided then and there she would put a stop to this. She turned and stepped toward the girls. Ava said "yes, I am in a gang and I will kick your ass if you ever say another word about me!" The girls stopped in their tracks. Ava had never stood up to them. As they looked at each other Ava continued, "the scar on my face that you're always cracking jokes about, it was my initiation, so you better watch your back from now on." The girls suddenly turned and walked quickly in the other direction. The scar on her face was from a car accident from when she was too young to remember and she had never been near any gangs. Still, she noticed that the girls began to avoid her, and others began giving her a wide berth.

With a little reprieve from the bullying, Ava began to relax at school. She began sitting outside on a bench in the courtyard. One day she noticed a boy coming out of the side door to the building. He was tall, with a short, neat haircut and a high yellow complexion. He smiled briefly at her as he walked by. Weeks passed and Ava would notice him in the halls when she went to her locker. They began to wave shyly at each other as they walked past. Ava had developed a slight crush. She did not dare try to speak to him out of fear. What if he rejected her too? What if he was just being nice by waving at her in the halls? Ava was not about to add that to the list of daily humiliations. Still, it would be nice to finally have someone to talk to at school. Ava let herself daydream about him when she was sitting in English Lit. She wished he would say hello to her, but she knew that would never happen to a girl like her. All the other girls said she was skinny and ugly anyway. She should not set herself up for the failure.

One day, the boy walked closer to Ava than usual and put a folded note on top of her books. Ava was so surprised she just stared after him as he went into the wide doors of the band hall. That was her next class, so she knew she would see him later. She tucked the letter into her literature book and headed off to class.

The handsome guy was named Scott and he was in the same grade as Ava. She did not know how she had never noticed him before. Ava could not wait to read the note, but she knew she could not let the other kids see her reading it. Someone would notice and try to take it away to share with the whole class. Everyone would have a good laugh at her expense.

Ava excused herself from class with the note now tucked into her hand. She went to the girl's bathroom. She went into the last stall and locked the door. Ava unfolded the short note. Scott had asked her to become his girlfriend! Ava was in shock. She could not believe what was written on the paper, so she read it again and again. She finally began to believe what she had read and realized she had to hurry back to class. She needed to write him a note to pass to him when they met outside the band hall today. She would have to hurry and make sure no one saw her write the note. But wait, what if they saw her give it to him? That would be disastrous. Ava had to come up with a plan. Finally, she figured out what to do. She would ask his friend Troy to give it to him instead. She would see him in the hall soon. She would make sure Troy did not let anyone else see the note, only Scott.

The note was delivered by the end of the day and Ava was excited. She had told Scott that she would like that very much, so she supposed it was official. The two were a couple. They were still very shy but somehow Scott found the courage to speak to her the next day. The moment was brief, and neither could remember what was said. Ava just remember the butterflies that danced in her stomach as she watched him walk away. That night Scott was all she could think about. She wondered what he liked to eat and what music he listened to. She wondered if he liked sports. Ava loved to watch the Boston Celtics and the Chicago Bulls. Did Scott have a favorite team? She hoped they could talk on the phone soon. Tomorrow she would slip him her phone number and ask him to call since there was no way they could talk at school.

The next day Ava had her note ready to give to Troy so that he could deliver it to Scott. She was in English Lit waiting for the bell and could barely contain her excitement. She kept finding a small smile playing at the edge of her lips at random moments. She let herself imagine how Scott's lips would feel against hers. Would he ask her out? She would love to see him after school, but she knew her father would never let that happen. Not after what had happened with Donnie.

The bell finally rang, and Ava grabbed her books and headed towards the band hall. As usual, she was pushed along with the tide of students going that direction. When she got closer, the double doors to the band hall swung outward with force, as though someone had slammed into it. A moment later, Scott emerged, and he did not look happy at all. There was a scowl on his face, and he was walking extremely fast, trying to get away from the other students coming behind him. Ava caught snatches of chatter and knew that they had found out. Scott came over to her and handed her a letter. Ava had a bad feeling. She went into the classroom and put the letter inside of her book along with the one she had written earlier. She would not read it until she was on the bus. The day was nearly over, and she would not have to worry about prying eyes.

Class ended and Ava was on the way to the bus. The walkway stretched the length of the line of buses and hers was at the other end. There were not many people nearby and Ava could not take the suspense a moment longer. She unfolded the letter. Scott said he had changed his mind and did not want to be her boyfriend. Again, he kept it short. Ava did not need an explanation. She had known the moment the band hall doors flew open and she saw him storm out. The other kids had made fun of him for liking her, the school pariah. He chose to end their newly formed friendship to get them off his back. Ava could not blame him.

Ava was disappointed and felt the familiar surge of shame. She stared out of the bus window not seeing anything they drove past. When she got home, she went to her room and cried. She did not feel sorry for herself, she just needed to release it all. She had feelings of anger at the kids who kept tormenting her. She was sad that she could not keep a friend.

She was angry at herself for daring to get her hopes up that a boy could like her. She felt that no matter what she did, she would always be alone. She felt that she would never be good enough. Deep down inside, she knew she did not deserve anything more. Ava just wanted to be ok with that.

CHAPTER 25
GROWING UP

Ava could not seem to shake her timid nature. She still had no friends, but plenty of cousins she could talk to if she chose. She hardly ever did. She had her books and writing to keep her company, so she rarely felt alone. She had stopped going to church regularly, suddenly developing tummy aches when it was time to leave for services. She loved her little nephew Michael and was good at taking care of him. He was the sweetest little one year old. He would watch everything going on in the house as though he knew and understood. He was the most intelligent baby Ava had ever known. Sometimes she took him with her on her walks. She went only to visit her Grandma and Grandpa some days after school.

One such Friday evening in April 1990, she decided to do just that. She left home and began walking down the road. Ava's family now lived just half a mile down the road on the same street as the rest of Jenney's family. The short walk only took a few minutes. When she got to the house, Ava's Grandma, aunties, and cousins were sitting on the front porch. Her aunts took her to the side and told her they were coming to get her the next day and they had a surprise for her.

They picked her up around six the next evening. It was still hot as the sun was blazing late into the spring days. As they began the drive, they told her it was time she started acting like an adult. They said she was no longer a child, so she needed to learn how to have a little fun. They said she was too shy and afraid of everything, so it was time for a change. They took her to a party on a street just up the road. They could not even park close to the house because there were so many cars on the street. They had to walk about a hundred yards to the house. People were milling around all over. Some were dancing to the music being blasted from a set of tall black speakers they had set up outside. The partygoers varied in age. There were older adults in their thirties to sixties and people as young as thirteen. Everyone looked like they were having fun.

Even though she knew most of the party goers, Ava was awkward and reserved, so she did not feel like mingling. Her aunts said she needed to loosen up and began plying her with alcohol. They gave her a cup of MD 20/20 and told her to finish it. Ava began drinking. Pretty soon she started to loosen up. Ava walked back to the line of cars alone, just to get a moment to herself. Her head was starting to spin. A few long moments passed, and a boy walked over to her. His name was Grant and even Ava had to admit he was cute. He was about 5'11", dark, and very muscular. His tank top revealed that he worked out quite often. Ava thought she must be drunk.

Grant said he liked her and would like to talk to her sometime. He asked if he could take her on a date. Ava was not allowed to date or party since the last few incidents went horribly wrong, so she told him she would have to ask her dad. Grant said that was fine, he would speak to her dad himself. Ava was in shock.

On the way home Ava's head was spinning and she felt sick

to her stomach. Her aunts instructed her to go straight to her room and not to speak to anyone. They told her she might have a stomachache and they did not want her throwing up in front of her parents. Ava did not want any trouble with Carl and the last thing she wanted was to see Jenney's disappointed expression. She did as they instructed.

The next day Grant showed up at the house around noon. He knocked on the door and Carl went to answer. Grant said, "hello sir I am Grant and I would like your permission to date your daughter." Carl began to close the door in Grant' face. Grant said, "excuse me sir, but can we step outside and talk for a minute?" Carl looked back at Ava and told her to stay inside. Ava was mortified. She imagined all sorts of ways that talk could go wrong. She decided she had better listen at the window to see if she heard raised voices or gunshots. To her surprise, the conversation must have gone well because when it ended, Grant had permission to take Ava on a date. That date turned into many more and soon the two were an item.

Over the next several weeks, Grant became a regular at Ava's house. Her father seemed to like him more than he liked his own daughters. Ava suspected he had secretly wanted a son and that Grant was filling that void. He would take him out and show him how to drive his Peterbilt. They spent time outside working on cars or washing them on weekends.

Grant began coming to the high school to pick Ava up at the end of each day. She was surprised when he would meet her in the gym. He would give her a hug and a peck on the cheek, then carry her books to the car. Ava just smiled as they walked away holding hands. Inside she was a mess. Her emotions were all over the place. She loved the attention Grant was showering on her, but she was terrified that it would not last. She was afraid to let him see how much she liked him. Each time he came to the school, she was scared the other kids would talk him out of seeing her. Grant guessed her thoughts and told her he did not care what anyone thought, he liked her, and no one could change that. Ava began to let her guard down.

Grant showed so much interest in Ava that she began to forget some of her earlier rules. She forgot to be afraid. He got her to try going to church again, consistently. While Ava had grown up in a non-denominational church, this was Grant' first time. He quickly got used to the lack of instrumental music and the less animated style of preaching. He encouraged Ava to take an offer she had received to teach a Sunday school class for the little kids. She thought it over and realized she needed to make peace with her faith.

She allowed herself to consider the possibility that God had not totally abandoned her. She began to let go of some of her fears. Love and acceptance were having a healing effect on her. Grant was so enthralled with the Gospel that he decided to get baptized and make the church his new priority. Each Sunday, he picked Ava up and they attended Sunday services. They sat next to each other in church, holding hands and staring at the preacher.

Each night they could not keep their hands to themselves. They knew they would have to choose. Fornication was wrong, but they were young and in love. Ava could not bear the thought of losing him. She did not know what to do. They sat down and spoke with their pastor who told them what they already knew.

They agreed to stop having sex.

CHAPTER 26
FATHERS AND DAUGHTERS

Grant and Ava went to the movies one cool May evening. They watched Beauty and the Beast and thought it was a great movie. After the movie, they picked up food from McDonalds and ate it on the way home. Ava still had to make her curfew of 11:00 p.m. Still, Grant stopped the car on a secluded dirt road as Ava had hoped he would. They began kissing and soon things began to get heated. Grant unzipped his pants and Ava dared to touch him. Grant thought it was a sign, so he began to push her head down to his lap. Ava resisted, and moved away, sliding back onto the passenger seat. All she could see was the old, nasty paraplegic pushing the back of her head. She did not want to ruin their date, so she pretended she was not feeling well. She asked Grant to take her home. He never knew the internal battle she was facing. Pulse racing, heart pounding, Ava closed her eyes and willed her breathing to slow. She wanted to tell Grant the truth about her, but the words refused to come. She was afraid he would not be able to look at her the same.

They sat in the car in the front yard for a few minutes when they got back to Ava's house. The house was dark, so they thought the family was asleep. Moments later, the door flew open and Vanessa came running to the car. She banged on the window on the passenger side, and Ava rolled it down. Vanessa told them "do not go in the house, no matter what!" She seemed frantic and upset. She started stomping up the dark road towards Grandma's house. Worried, Ava jumped out of the car and ran up the steps and through the door. Jenney was sitting in the dark, crying and wringing her hands. "What's the matter mama," Ava said as she dropped to her knees in front of her mom. Jenney sobbed louder. Ava was frightened. She had not seen her mom so upset in years, not since she had stopped partying and drinking. She could not imagine what could be wrong. Ava wrapped her arms around her mother and said, "it's going to be alright mom, I love you very much!" Jenney pushed Ava off her and screamed into her face, "don't ever say those words to me, it's all lies. Your dad said the same words and look what he's done." "Mama, what's going on, what are you talking about, of course I love you," Ava said. Jenney's eyes grew hard and she began to speak. "I caught your father having sex with Vanessa, his own daughter! After I caught them, he told me he loves her."

Ava could not believe her ears. She got to her feet and slowly began backing away. Her hands covered her mouth of their own will. She was staring at her mom but did not see her. As the words reverberated around her mind, Ava felt trapped inside the small house. She reached the door and felt as though an invisible hand was squeezing her heart, making it hard to breathe. Ava ran outside and down the street; the opposite way Vanessa had gone. She ran past the yard where their neighbor D. C. had lived for years. Tears blinded her. Grant caught up to her before she got to the next house and tried to make her stop running. Ava kept moving and finally stopped in front of the cemetery. She was completely disgusted. Why would Carl do such a deplorable thing? How could he possibly think of his own daughter that way? Surely, he knew how awful that was! Grant asked her what was going on, but she was too ashamed to tell. She sobbed and hugged herself and told Grant to leave her alone. He refused and just pulled her gently into his strong arms. Ava dissolved into a wailing mess of gut-wrenching sobs. Grant held her until she was quiet. She moved away from him slightly and continued walking down the street. When they were under the hill, she told him what she had learned. She told him her whole family was seriously messed up. She told him that she had been raped by one family member, still unable to speak of the others. Now she was confronted with Carl's disgusting behavior. Her whole family was deviant. She expected Grant to leave her right then. Who would want her after hearing that her family was capable of such depravity? She certainly could not imagine that he would want to stay after that. After she told him Ava felt a pain grip her insides. She doubled over and retched as her dinner found its way out once again. Ava could not stop shaking. Her mind was at once denying the reality of what her father had done and envisioning the two of them together. Her sister and her father.

Grant took her hand and put a finger under her chin. He told her to look into his eyes. She resisted at first, dropping her gaze to the paved road, but he gently lifted her to face his. He said he would always love and protect her. Nothing else mattered and no one could change that. Ava paused, looking at him deeply, searching for signs he was lying. After everything in her past, how could she allow herself to believe him? What if all men were as awful as the ones who had hurt her? What if they were all like her dad? Ava looked for the lies in Grant's eyes again. Finding nothing but sincerity, she threw her arms around his neck, grateful that he had so much courage. Loving a thing as broken as her could not be easy. Tonight's events seemed to prove that beyond a shadow of a doubt.

Ava refused to go back inside her house. The place seemed

tainted after that. She walked back to Grant's car and told him to drive to his house. Grant drove them to his place that he shared with his brother and his brother's wife. He led Ava to his bedroom at the back. Ava got into his bed and Grant stood next to her. He placed the covers over her and then sat on top of the blankets. He lay next to Ava and held her in his arms. Ava cried softly, her body still trembling. She was in a state of disbelief. As her tears fell silently, Ava began to remember. She remembered waking up one night when she was in her bed in the room she and Elena shared with Vanessa. She was irritated at whatever had awakened her. She looked over and saw Vanessa sitting up in her bed, her head resting against the wall. The mysterious sound came again. Her father was standing outside of their room, calling out to Vanessa. He was asking her to come out of the room, saying "I just want to talk." Vanessa had turned over in her bed, placing her back to the door. Their father had called out to her once more, and Vanessa made a frustrated sound. She stomped onto the floor and jerked the bedroom door open. Angry that they had awakened her, Ava had turned over and gone back to sleep.

Fresh tears began coursing down her face as she began to understand. The two had either been having a lover's quarrel, or her father had been trying to convince Vanessa to have sex with him again. Ava felt sick again. She was totally disgusted. How had she not noticed this was going on? She could not believe she had been so blind. She had not suspected a thing.

Ava cried herself to sleep as Grant held her through the night. When she woke up suddenly from her troubled sleep, he kissed her on the forehead and murmured softly until she was sleeping again. He did not leave her side until Ava awakened the next morning.

Jenney made Carl leave the house, but he came back a few weeks later. Jenney could not pay the bills on her own, so she needed his income. By now, the whole neighborhood was talking about what Carl had done. Ava knew her mother did not want to be in the same house with her dad and frankly neither did she. Jenney had never held down a job, so she had no hope of paying the bills. Life seemed unfair. Jenney had worked hard to turn her life around. She had given up the party life and stopped drinking all on her own several years before. Even though Carl had stopped his physical assaults years earlier, Jenney was constantly at his mercy. Carl was controlling. He gave Jenney money to pay bills and for the things he approved only. He would yell at her and curse her out violently if she put too much salt in his food or did not add ice to his drink. Carl berated Jenney every chance he got. Jenney was not as close to her mom and sisters because Carl did not approve of her spending time with them when he was not around. Jenney began to slowly let him take over every decision of her life. She did the cooking, cleaning, ironing, and still it had not been enough to keep Carl from straying.

Ava decided then and there that her father was the worst monster of all. All the years of ignoring her, beating Jenney, and telling them all how to live had been a facade. He went to church but smoked, he had beaten Ava for being raped, calling her ungodly names, and damning her to hell. The whole time he had been the devil, sleeping with his own daughter. The betrayal cut deeply. Jenney had spent years getting her life in order and this was how he thanked his wife. The betrayal to his family was glaring. Still the hypocrisy was worse. Demanding so much from others while indulging in depravity was surely a worse kind of sin. Ava wanted nothing more to do with such a man. She no longer considered him her father.

The deacons at church made them come in for a meeting. They began counseling sessions with Ava's parents. Ava did not hold back her feelings. She told the pastor that her father had betrayed his whole family that he was a complete disgrace. She had lost any respect she once had for him. The pastor told Ava that she should forgive her father. He said she needed to understand that Carl had never seen Vanessa as his child. He said since he had never raised her, he only saw her as a woman. He said Vanessa had seduced Carl and that she was just as much to blame. Ava wanted to believe that, and she would for years, until Jenney finally told her the family secret.

CHAPTER 27
RELATIONS

The family seemed a hollow shell of itself a few weeks later. Carl tried to avoid everyone in the house. He and Jenney shared the same bed each night, but their days were filled with a tense silence. Jenney had insisted that Vanessa move out, but somehow, she was still in the house.

Vanessa began spending more and more time at Grandma Nancy's house. Ava could not comprehend why. She knew Vanessa wanted to get away from the tension at home, but Ava could not fathom why she did not just move out altogether. She still had family in Mobile that could take her in or at least help her find her own place. Still, Ava was not entirely comfortable with that idea either because it would mean Vanessa would take Michael with her. Neither Ava nor Elena could bear the thought of being separated from their nephew. He seemed almost angelic to them and his aunts were completely enthralled.

One Saturday in January, sixteen-year-old Ava walked into Grandma Nancy's yard and saw Vanessa leaving from the back door. That room was her brother Jimmy's. Why was Vanessa in there? She knew Vanessa had not slept at home because her bed was still made this morning. She had seen her leave after dark, walking up the dark street.

When Ava got home, she told her mother what she had seen. Jenney said nothing. The next day, Carl was livid and began cursing at Vanessa. They took their argument outside. A few weeks passed and Ava noticed Vanessa was out of the house once again. She thought she had a good idea of where she was. She saw Vanessa later that day when she got to her Grandma's house. No longer attempting to hide their affair, Jimmy and Vanessa were sitting next to each other.

The mood in Ava's family home was even more intense. Vanessa had slept with Jenney's husband, her own father and now she was sleeping with Jenney's son. Carl was clearly upset and feeling somehow betrayed by the affair. Ava and Elena were embarrassed and tried to avoid the whole sordid mess.

After a few months, Jenney noticed Vanessa's stomach was quite swollen. She was wearing a loose dress, but the jacket over it had flapped in the wind. Vanessa was heavily pregnant. Jenney was enraged. She told Carl to get Vanessa out of her house immediately. Ava and Elena went to school and returned to find Vanessa gone. Her bags were all gone and nothing of hers remained. To the girls' surprise she did leave one thing behind. Michael was playing on the couch and both girls ran to him and gave him hugs.

Ava thought things were finally looking up. They settled into a routine of caring for Michael when they came home from school. They took turns feeding, bathing, and clothing him and played with him every day. They began teaching him small words, and Michael would repeat them. He even picked up the alphabet before his third birthday. The girls would go to school and wait anxiously for the moment they got home to play with their nephew.

CHAPTER 28
BROTHERS

One evening in late September, the family was sitting at home and the phone rang. It was Vanessa on the other line. She had given birth to a son who was almost a month old. Her voice carried over the phone line and Ava could hear her say, "come get this boy because my boyfriend doesn't like him." The family piled into the car and drove straight to Mobile the same night. Vanessa had apparently returned there earlier in the month.

They located the address she had given them over the phone. It led them to a rundown apartment complex. They all went inside and were immediately overcome by the smell of urine and human feces. The elevator doors stood open, obviously defunct as old furniture and pieces of wood littered the car. There was garbage piled high all around and they had to pick their way through. Some numbers were on the doors that still stood. They walked up the cement steps, careful to avoid the debris. When they got to the third floor, the amount of garbage doubled, and the awful odors threatened to take their breath away. Everyone tucked their nose inside their shirts or jackets as they inched towards the last apartment on the left.

Finally finding their destination, Ava was dismayed. The door to the apartment had been broken down and lay splintered in a jagged heap. Dirty diapers trailed a path into the living room. Vanessa was sitting on a filthy floor and her boyfriend was across from her. The baby was in another room and Carl went to get him. They had heard his cries from down the hall, but no one in the room seemed to notice. When Carl emerged with the screaming baby, he was covered in his own hardened feces. It was eerily apparent that the diaper had not been changed in days. The baby was crying because he was filthy, hungry, and sick.

With bugs and roaches crawling all around the place, Ava's family left with the baby and his legal papers, no clothes, formula, or diapers. They went to the nearest corner store and purchased what they could. They sat in the parking lot and used bottled water to loosen the hardened feces from the baby's skin. They put on a fresh diaper and gave him formula they had just bought from the gas station. The baby was wrapped in someone's jacket, they would have to wait until morning to buy him clothes.

The girls could not sleep on the ride back home. The events of the night weighed too heavily. The poor little baby was quiet now, having had something to quell his hunger. They found his name on the papers Vanessa had sent with him. Little Dylan was a handsome baby, but he would need plenty of love and attention. The irony of the situation was not lost on anyone, though no one dared to mention it. Vanessa had not only had a sexual relationship with her father, she had been sleeping with Jenney's son at the same time. Now, they were going to raise both of her children, despite the rift it had left in their home.

When they got home, they gave Dylan a bath in warm soapy water. They let him sit in the water for long moments, splashing as he worked his little legs. Afterwards, they wrapped him in a warm towel and diapered him once again. The baby slept soundly.

Jenney came back the next morning with clothes, formula, and other necessities. The family took Dylan to Grandma Nancy's. The adults talked and agreed that Dylan would stay there. The brothers would not grow up in the same house, despite Ava's wishes. Ava suspected there was more going on than she and Elena were privy to. Still, Dylan would remain with her mother's family.

Although the girls visited with Dylan nearly every day, they felt deprived. They had such a strong bond with Michael because he lived in the same house. They knew his every need, every cry, and were there to cater to him at a moment's notice. Their connection increased every day. Dylan was not growing up in their home, so their bond was considerably hampered. Still, they remained close and made sure the boys were raised as brothers.

CHAPTER 29
SHATTERED

A year later, they were not prepared for the shock one evening after school. Ava and Elena came bursting through the doors after getting off the school bus. Both ran inside looking for Michael, but he was not there. Jenney came from the bedroom and explained that Vanessa had shown up at the house. Jenney had no warning, but she had come for her son. She took him back with her to Dothan, Alabama, which was several hours away. Apparently, Vanessa's mother had been living there for years. Vanessa was staying with her and her live-in boyfriend, and now Michael was there with them too.

Ava and Elena stared at each other in disbelief. How could this be true? Both girls were nearly hysterical and dissolved into tears. The pain was almost a thing they could touch, it cut them so deeply. The two sisters were inconsolable and begged Jenney to go get Michael and bring him back. They could not go on without him in their lives. He was their light and their hope, all innocent and sweet. He was everything to them and they could not imagine their lives without him. Jenney said that was not possible, because legally, Vanessa had all the rights to take her child wherever she wanted. There was nothing any of them could do. Ava was angry and hurt and so was Elena. Ava screamed that Vanessa had ruined their whole family. Ever since the day she came into their lives, there seemed to be nothing but pain. She wished she had never heard Vanessa's name. Ava and Elena hugged each other and cried as the reality set in. Their sweet nephew Michael was lost to them.

Days seemed gloomy and both teenagers carried a weight of sadness and despair. Each day seemed to pass more slowly than ever, stretching into weeks of bitter regret. The girls missed Michael with a visceral, gut-wrenching pain. His removal from their lives was so abrupt, they had not been given a chance to say goodbye. That was the worst part. Ava wondered if Michael was ok. Were they treating him well? Was he missing his aunts as they were missing him?

Two months went by and it seemed as though it had been two years. As they were sitting on the evening bus about to go home from school, a girl named Eve said, "Ava, Michael is back." Ava was about to curse her for everything she could think of for playing such a mean, cruel prank. Eve pointed down at the car parked in the grass beside their bus. Jenney was there, sitting in the driver's seat and right next to her was their nephew! Ava grabbed her books and nearly took flight as she descended the school bus steps. She could not believe her eyes. Michael was there in the car with Mama. She saw Elena running towards the car too, and they reached it at the same moment. Both girls got into the front seat, crying tears of joy. They grabbed their nephew and showered him with hugs and covered his handsome face with kisses. He politely hugged them back but said nothing.

That night the family celebrated with a big meal at home. Everyone was laughing and smiling and doting on Michael. The girls gave him his bath, letting him play in the tub. Ava noticed he was still incredibly quiet and answered each question with a serenity and calmness that belied his short years. His usual youthful energy seemed to be checked. When the girls asked questions of Michael, he replied in a clipped, proper speech a simple "yes" or "no." It was as if he had been coached to only speak when spoken to and to deliver precise answers. Michael stared straight ahead and did not seek engagement. Ava thought it was odd, but they put Michael to bed.

In the middle of the night Michael woke with a blood curdling scream that jolted everyone in the house out of their sleep. Ava and Elena ran to him immediately. Michael was inconsolable. Still trapped in his nightmare, he began to sob and fight, hitting at the air above him. Everyone was shaken, knowing that Michael was not fully awake and trapped in his bad dream. They called his name and lightly tapped his face to try to wake him fully. Finally, Michael's eyes focused and he began to speak. He said monsters were chasing him in his head and they were going to get him. The two- year- old cried and said he wished he were dead. The family exchanged glances, shocked at the grown -up words coming from his two -year- old lips. Ava could not believe it. She thought she recognized the fear and the helplessness she was witnessing. In her heart, she believed something bad had happened to her nephew to cause this intense nightmare. She grabbed him and tried to comfort him, but he pushed her away. Ava gave him his space, but she stayed home the next day. She refused to leave his side. She began spending all her time talking to Michael. She kept showering him with love and affection until he started to interact again. Soon he started to laugh and play as he once had. Ava felt and saw him becoming his fun-loving self once again.

A few months had passed since Michael came home and things were settling into a routine of their own. Carl was driving trucks. His loads took him away from home during the week and he came home on weekends. Jenney was usually cooking and doing word search puzzles and enjoying her church activities. She never missed a Sunday or Wednesday evening service. She would spend some of Carl's paycheck to buy nice dresses and shoes, so she always looked nice for church.

CHAPTER 30
HEALING

Ava did not realize that helping her nephew was also healing for her. She began to feel more at ease within herself and her confidence in her abilities grew. She was just a year away from graduating high school and she and Grant were still an item. In fact, they were closer than ever. She began to think about her future.

Ava went to see the school guidance counselor for the very first time. She learned that she had maintained a near perfect GPA for her entire high school journey. The counselor said she should consider going to college. She found out the high school had a program called dual enrollment. She signed up for a college class two nights per week. She found the work no more challenging than high school, but it was stimulating just the same. Ava was enjoying this new phase of life.

Being loved had a positive effect on Ava. She was finally starting to feel like a normal life could be in her future. She was very much in love with Grant and they spent all their spare time together. He took her everywhere he went. They went fishing with his mother and brother several times. Ava found that she loved it. Grant would take her to softball games at the park in the small town he grew up, just seven miles away. The park would fill with people from all around and the tournaments would last for hours. At night, Ava and Grant would give in and make love despite their promises before.

She would go to church and silently pray for forgiveness. She knew that what they were doing was wrong. Grant began to stay home on some Sundays, so Ava would go with her parents. She worked with the younger kids at church teaching the stories she had memorized long ago. Ava found healing in teaching others about the path to salvation. She wanted to continue to grow. Her nightmares began to dissipate and soon she was feeling a sense of peace. She felt closer to God on a spiritual level and allowed her faith to flourish. Ava made friends at her church, people she had now gotten to know. Still, she knew she would have to make some changes, or all her work would mean nothing. She would have to tell Grant.

CHAPTER 31
A DREAM DEFERRED

Ava loved every moment with both the boys and would seek them out when she was not in school. She loved her college classes also, and the interactions with the other students. She still struggled to overcome her shy nature, but soon began to answer questions when the professor asked. She challenged herself to do so to try to get over her anxiety.

Mere weeks into her first semester, Grant began to complain. He dropped her off at the community college and came back when class ended to pick her up. Some days class did not end on time and Grant would wait outside in the car. One evening on the drive home Grant was quiet. Ava was excited about what she had just learned and was telling him all about it. Grant sat silently. Ava realized he was upset. She asked, "baby what's your problem tonight, what's going on?" Grant put both hands onto the steering wheel and kept his gaze straight ahead. Ava stared at him expectantly. Finally, Grant stiffly replied "I don't like you being at that school. I think you need to quit." Ava was astonished. She said, "why do you want me to quit, I thought you were on board with me going to school?" Grant raised his voice slightly, "I said you need to quit. There are too many fools running in and out that place. I don't like you being in there with them." Ava laughed lightly, "is that all, babe? You're worried I might find someone else? You know I only have eyes for you." She reached out to stroke his cheek and Grant flinched away. He said "you need to choose. It's either school or me. You cannot have both." Ava was instantly angry. She started yelling and asking him how he could say something like that. Was her future not as important as his? They lapsed into silence and he refused to give an answer. When they got to her house, Grant dropped her off and left. He did not return for several days and refused to take Ava's calls.

Ava was conflicted. She loved Grant with all her heart, and she wanted to be with him; but how could he make her choose between a better future and him? If she did not do something, she would end up stuck in this little town with no hope for a decent life. Ava wanted to become a psychologist and Grant had said he supported that. They had agreed that school was a good choice for their future together. They would have a better chance if she had a college education. Now that she was doing something to further that goal, he seemed to be bailing on her. She had tried telling him how unfair that was, but he was not hearing her out. He was only concerned with keeping her to himself. Ava just could not let that happen. She began getting her mom to take her to classes and tried to forget about how much Grant had hurt her.

A few weeks had gone by and he still would not return her calls. Saturday came and Ava decided to go to the softball game at the park. She hoped it would take her mind off Grant. She drove to the park in the Pontiac she shared with Elena. She parked just outside the gate. There were lines of cars on both sides of the entrance to the park and all the spots inside were filled. As she walked into the park, she saw a few of the girls from her school stealing glances at her. Ava did not know why.

As she got closer, she saw Grant sitting in his car with another girl. She knew her from school as well. Ava turned around and started back to her car. The girls snickered as she walked by. She felt her cheeks go hot and her eyes welled with tears. She refused to let them see her cry. She kept her head up and forced her steps to slow as she continued. As soon as she got into the car, the dam broke. She had not realized she had been holding her breath until it came in a rush. Her shoulders shook as guttural sobs left her body. She felt her whole world spinning. She stayed there for long moments, with her hands on the wheel as the tears refused to stop. Eventually, she was calm enough to drive away. Hot tears still streaked her face and she felt hollow inside, in a state of disbelief. Her head felt ready to pop. Now she knew Grant was seeing someone and that was why he had not returned her calls. She had been replaced.

Ava began having trouble sleeping. She seemed to be crying all the time. She missed Grant, but he had hurt her. She felt betrayed and mocked because everyone had already known. Some of the girls at school were quick to rub it in. They had been jealous all along. Ava ignored their stares and jabs and avoided them altogether. She barely even registered their presence.

Grant came to see her the following Saturday. Ava met him outside the house. He asked her to get into the car to take a drive so they could talk. Ava refused. She told him she knew he was seeing someone, and Grant lied outright. She told him they had nothing more to talk about and turned to walk away. Grant grabbed her arm and turned her to face him. He said "ok you're right and I'm sorry. I should have told you. I'm sorry I lied." Ava said "is that all you're sorry for? You hurt me Grant and I don't know how to forgive you. You of all people should never have hurt me like that. You know what I've been through, how could you do that to me after everything we have been to each other?" Grant dropped his head and pulled Ava close to him. He said he would never treat her that way again. He told her they belonged together, and he would never stray if only she would take him back. Ava raised her arms to push him away and he grabbed her chin gently. Grant raised her face to his and kissed the tears away. He held her for a long moment and Ava felt her resistance begin to dissipate. She slowly returned his embrace. He kissed her lips this time and Ava kissed him back. They agreed to try once more.

Days later Ava asked for a ride to evening classes and Grant went still. He said "I thought you were done with that bullshit Ava. I thought we settled that." Ava dropped her head. She turned and walked back inside the house. She did not return to school.

CHAPTER 32

REVELATIONS

It was early in 1992 and Ava and her mom began to talk more often. They started slowly at first, but soon developed a mutual respect. Ava worked hard to make peace with the things she had endured and forgave her mother. She never discussed any of the events in question. She did not know how to tell her. She had no idea how much her mom may have known. She felt she would begin the conversation when the time seemed right.

As the two started getting closer, they would often shop and grab something to eat. One of their favorite places to eat was a little pizza place across the line in Mississippi. Ava, Jenney, and Elena had gone shopping one Saturday to get outfits for church. After shopping, they pulled into the parking lot of the pizza shop. Ava loved this place, but as soon as they went inside, she felt nausea begin to build. She tried to ignore it. The restaurant was buffet style, so they all fixed their favorites. Ava piled her plate high with salad and drizzled on her favorite ranch dressing. They sat at their table to eat and suddenly Ava became ill. She ran to the bathroom and threw up violently. She cleaned up and returned to the table. Again, the smells of the food were an assault on her senses, and Ava could stand it no longer. She asked Jenney for the car keys and left her food untouched on the table. She got into the backseat and lay down. The queasiness seemed to pass before Jenney and Elena returned to the car.

Jenney got inside and started the engine. She looked at Ava in the rearview mirror. "I'm taking you to the pharmacy, young lady," said Jenney. With a prophetic and disapproving smile, she continued, "I hope you know you're pregnant." Ava laughed out loud.

A few minutes after arriving home mom told her how to take the test they had stopped for. Ava was more afraid than she could have predicted. There was no way she was ready to have a baby. How would she continue school? Would she get to finish college? What about Grant, would he stand by her, or would this be the moment he finally chose to leave? What if he left her? How would she raise a child on her own? She had no means of supporting herself, let alone a little person. How did she let this happen? She must have been out of her mind. It could not be, it simply could not happen. She was not pregnant. There was simply no way that could be the case.

Still, she took the test. Within seconds two lines appeared on the stick.

Nineteen-year-old Ava was going to have a baby.

CHAPTER 33
GOODBYES

In December of 1992, Ava gave birth to a healthy baby boy. She had passed out after the birth and woke to find that he had been given a name. Grant Jr. came home to eager family members from both sides ready to spoil and love him. Even girls from her school stopped by to see Grant Jr. cooing and fawning over him. Ava was quite protective, never allowing anyone to step out of her sight when they were holding her baby. She wanted to protect him from any possible harm. Ava decided that nursing her sweet son was best. The moments she spent catering to him created an unmistakable bond.

Grant had proven to be reliable, staying by her side throughout the pregnancy. He made a point of rubbing her back and feet when she felt tired or strained. They began to make plans for a future together, to make a family for their son. Grant wanted the two of them to marry and make their new life official. Ava began to dream again. She had visions of a long happy life with her son and Grant, but she was not sure she wanted to marry. She had such poor examples; she did not want to end up like that. She wanted their child to grow up happy and safe.

Ava began taking her son out of the house. She never wanted to be away from him. She took him to football games even though he was too little to enjoy it at all. She enjoyed every moment with him. She felt that she finally had found the purpose her life was previously missing. She wanted to make sure her son had all the opportunities she never did.

Grant would stay over many nights to help care for their son. He loved him and doted on him almost as much as Ava did. He brought his friends over and took Grant Jr. outside to meet them. He smiled down at him with such pride. Ava would watch them from the window in her bedroom, making sure they were careful not to let him fall.

Grant and Ava loved watching their son grow and learn. Ava felt like she was seeing the world for the first time. When Grant Jr. learned to walk, Ava was ecstatic, but sad that his father had missed his first steps. She called him over, but Grant did not answer. It was hours before he came. Ava felt something was wrong, because Grant never missed an opportunity to spend time with his son. She finally heard his car pulling into the yard. She left the baby inside and met Grant outside.

Grant was clearly anxious and more than a little drunk. He reached to grab Ava's hand. She quickly moved out of his reach and asked where he had been. Grant told Ava he was sorry, but he was leaving town in less than a week. He was moving to New Jersey. His older sister was going to help him find work there, so he was not planning to return. Ava was silent, in shock, wondering what would become of their family. She asked him to consider their future. Was he leaving them behind for good? Grant said "no, one day I will come back?" Ava noticed that he did not say he was coming for her or for their child. She felt her pulse begin to race. Tears welled in her eyes and spilled down her face, but Grant did not seem disturbed. He was cold to her. Distant. Almost uncaring. Ava had no idea what had changed. She looked at the man she loved so much and saw a stranger staring back at her. Grant reached for her and gave her a hug as Ava began to sob. His quick hug lasted just an instant and he turned to walk back to his car. Ava stood there, crying, feeling abandoned and afraid. She watched him reverse out of the yard and onto the narrow street. He turned and looked at her once and gave a small wave of goodbye.

CHAPTER 34
SPIRAL

Her parents had begun helping much more than Ava could ever have hoped for. Carl bought a small mobile home and set it up for Ava and her son. Ava could not believe he had done that. She was still wary of him, but grateful that he had gotten her a place of her own. The house was situated on Carl's property, so it was just down the street. Carl had paid to have the land prepared for the mobile home to sit so that they did not share a yard. Ava could still see their house from the window in the front bedroom, so was not afraid of living there alone. She and Grant Jr. had their own space.

Carl and Jenney were enthralled with Grant Jr. They began taking him with them every time they went out. They took him fishing and to visit with family and their friends. It gave Ava some time alone.

Grant had been gone for almost four months and Ava had only received a few calls. She was caring for her son without his father, but it still felt surreal. She had to learn to take care of herself and her child without him. She missed him more than she could have imagined. Ava began to revert to her old solitary behavior. She stopped visiting her family members and stayed inside her house. She would take her son to her mom and come back to the trailer alone. She began to sleep through most of the day. She turned to books seeking the pleasure she always found between the pages of a good story but found she could no longer focus. Words on the page seemed to give her headaches each time she picked up a book. She stopped going for walks as she felt dazed when she was out on the street. She could not seem to pay attention to her surroundings. Ava could no longer engage with her little sister, with whom she had always shared a special bond. She rarely saw her sister and the worst part was that Ava barely even noticed.

Ava was distraught over losing Grant. She felt heartbroken and betrayed. He had always been so amazing to her and then he had just walked out. To make matters worse, he had left his only child behind as if he did not care for him at all. Was it all just lies? Had he ever genuinely cared? Ava was starting to doubt that he had. She cried herself to sleep night after night waiting for him to call. Ava could not eat and began to lose weight rapidly. She felt tired and drained nearly every day.

Ava was at home and someone began knocking on her door. It was the middle of the afternoon one Saturday in late June. Grant Jr. was with her parents as he often was of late. Ava reluctantly went to the door. A girl she had gone to school was there. She and Ava had spoken before and knew each other well. They were not close, but around the same age so they knew most of the same people. Her name was Rena and Ava invited her in. They began talking and Rena told her she was about to get dressed to go out to a nightclub later that evening. She invited Ava to join her. Ava was not in the mood and Rena said that was fine, but she wanted to get her out of the house just the same. Rena lived just down the street and would often see Ava when she passed the house. She reached over and pulled Ava from her chair and jokingly convinced her to get dressed. Ava complied to get her to be quiet. Her voice was making Ava's headache worse, so she got up and went to her room. She found some shorts and a tank top and headed for the shower.

Later, they got into the car that Carl had given Ava and Elena and drove to a nearby town. Ava knew the lady who lived there. Her name was Dean and she had quite a reputation for drinking, fighting, and partying. At first, Ava was afraid to get out of the car because she and Dean had never spoken. Rena reminded her that Dean was family, they were all related to Grant. Ava relented and went with Rena to the open door of the wooden house. As soon as she walked in a chorus of "what's up" embraced Rena. Ava was surprised that they spoke to her too. There were people all around and they welcomed Ava as if she had been there before. They greeted her as if she was a part of their clique. Dean was at the card table playing spades and she called Ava over to sit next to her. She asked her if she wanted a drink. Ava thought it over briefly and accepted a cold can of beer. Dean looked at her and smiled.

Ava had two more beers and joined the spades game. She was having fun with her newfound friends. They began to visit her at her house and took her out to all the clubs. Dean took Ava under her wing and did not let anyone threaten Ava. Ava began spending more time with her friends than she did at home with her son.

Soon, Ava was partying as if she was making up for lost time. She would find a different club to attend five nights of the week. She felt like a different person when she was out at the clubs. She could forget the pain of her past and pretend to forget Grant. That year, Ava learned she could dance. One night after a few drinks, Ava looked around the room. She was sitting at the table with her friends. She saw the same faces that she had come to know in the months she had been coming to the place. Ava realized she was incredibly bored. She desperately needed to stop her train of thoughts. She could feel herself becoming sad and missing Grant. Ava quickly downed her drink and took another to the crowded dance floor. She began to dance to the beat. She easily found a slow, steady rhythm and began to relax. She closed her eyes and willed her thoughts away. Ava began a slow grind and abandoned herself to the music. She felt as though she was floating. She held her cup in one hand and slowly raised the other into the air, her fingers weaving a dance of their own, keeping a sensual time with the beat. As Ava danced, she forgot to be sad. She felt her inhibitions float away. She could not feel any of the usual pain. She lost track of time. The music changed suddenly, and she opened her eyes. She sucked in a sharp breath as she looked around. The dance floor was nearly empty. Everyone was standing in a circle around it and all eyes were on her. She gasped out loud. Ava felt a jolt of the old fear from her high school days. She was sure they were all about to start pointing and laughing at any moment. She turned to leave and suddenly the girls she came out with came running to her side. They all embraced and began dancing next to her to the new, faster song. They began telling her she was a hit. All the guys were standing there drooling and the girls were all mad. Ava had stolen the show.

Ava began to party even more after that night. She would stay out later and later each time. She had taken a job to pay her own bills and would often go to work hung over. Some mornings she barely got home in time to shower and make the forty-five-minute drive to the sewing factory. She drank more and more, even at home. She only spent a small amount of time with her son. As Ava spiraled deeper out of control, she began to lose the bond with her only child.

One Saturday morning Ava walked to Grandma Nancy's. She had no other plans for the day. She wanted to spend some time just being lazy. She was sitting outside on the big porch when someone called Grandma Nancy's phone and asked for her. It was the girl down the street, Rena. She asked Ava to come ride with the crew to the softball field nearby. Ava was a little tired, but she told Rena to come pick her up. Suddenly, Ava remember something and dialed Rena back. She asked Rena who would be riding with them. Rena told her the names and Ava decided she had better take some protection with her. A girl named Shandi was going to be with them, and she seemed to hate Ava's guts. Each time they were near each other Shandi had something rude to say. Ava never missed an opportunity to give it right back, but she had learned she had to watch herself in Shandi's company. Shandi had a reputation for beating up other girls. Ava had seen her and her cousin double team another girl on the school bus once before. She knew the girl was brutal. Still Ava was not going to miss out on a day with her other friends just because of her.

They got to the field and Ava saw that there were several cars parked in a cluster. The field was otherwise empty. They pulled up and joined the group. There were about fifteen people milling around, sitting on their cars, and drinking ice cold beer. Ava recognized everyone there, they had gone to her high school. None of them had ever been kind to her, but they were all laughing and speaking with her as though they were the best of friends. Everyone was drinking and cracking jokes on each other. Shandi began calling Ava nasty names and Ava responded in kind. Shandi was standing a few feet away. She backed away a bit and Ava saw her throw a beer bottle just before it hit her in the face. Ava did not know why she did not flinch. She could have moved out of the way to avoid being hit. Instead she had stood there and watched it sail towards her. Ava calmly began walking forward, slowly with her eyes glued to Shandi. One of the guys grabbed Ava from behind and held her back and another boy helped him hold her. Shandi began to advance. Ava struggled to get free, thinking she was about to be beaten very badly, but Dean stepped in. She yelled at the boys to let Ava go and let this play out. None of them realized that Ava was no longer in control of herself. Ava walked forward and Shandi began to back away. Ava advanced on her more quickly. Shandi ran, backwards away from Ava. Ava blacked out. When she came out of her daze Rena was pulling her back and telling her to stop. She said, "you're going to kill her Ava stop it right now!" Ava focused on Rena's face and then looked over at Shandi. Shandi was being held up on her feet by two boys, one on either side of her. Ava had a short pocketknife in her hand and blood was dripping from it. Shandi had blood on her neck and dripping down her arm and her face had several scratches. Ava did not know what had happened. Rena and Dean took Ava to the car and shut her inside. They ushered the boys into a truck and instructed them to get Shandi to the hospital. The boys drove away with Shandi bleeding from the knife wounds Ava had inflicted. Rena was sitting next to Ava in the back seat of the car. She reached for Ava's hand. Ava flinched and almost hit her with the knife she had not known she was holding. Rena grabbed the knife and threw it out the car's window. She told Ava to look at her hand. Ava's hand had been sliced to the bone and the white flesh inside was hanging out. Ava could not feel a thing. Rena wanted to take Ava to the hospital, but Ava refused. She wanted to go home.

That night, Ava's mom came to her house and asked Ava what was going on. She said she was told there had been a stabbing in Shady Grove. Ava did not want to talk about it and Jenney backed off. As Jenney turned to walk out of the door, she suddenly exclaimed "Ava what happened to your hand, you are bleeding?" Dazed, Ava looked down. She saw blood dripping from her hand to the floor. Jenney grabbed her forearm and led her to the kitchen sink. She ran cold water onto her hand and lifted it higher so that she could examine it. "My God Ava you have to get this stitched up." Ava allowed her mom to drive her to Waynesboro, Mississippi to the hospital there. They went to the Emergency department. Ava was questioned by the attending physician due to the appearance of her injury. She lied and told him she had cut herself on a broken glass while doing dishes. Skeptical, the physician placed a long needle into the open wound of her hand. He said it would kill the pain. He began to sew the open wound from the inside first, placing three stitches. Ava could not feel any of it, but the doctor added more lidocaine. He then placed seven stitches to close the outer wound.

Back at her house, Ava could not go to sleep. She could not stop thinking of the events of the day. Ava did not know what had become of her. How had she become so angry and cold? She did not recognize herself anymore. She could have really hurt someone. What if Shandi's injuries were more severe than Ava knew? How badly was she hurt? Why could she not remember? Should Ava try to find out where they had taken her for treatment, or should she just stay home and wait? What if they had called the police. Ava could lose her son. She could go to jail or worse. What had she done?

Ava did not go to any parties or clubs for the next few weeks. She was afraid of what she had become. She remembered how she had felt so detached on the field that day. It was as if she were watching herself but had no control over her actions. She had not wanted to kill Shandi, but she had deliberately gone after her even when she was running the other way. She had felt a rage begin burning deep inside of her when Shandi began calling her names. As she watched the bottle coming for her face, it seemed as though time had slowed to a near crawl. Ava remembered feeling the rage explode throughout her mind and she ran after Shandi. Her mind had gone completely blank after that. She still could not recall how she got so far away from the cars. How had she caught up to Shandi? How many blows had Shandi suffered before they pulled Ava off her? Ava had no memory of those moments and it frightened her tremendously. Who knew what she was capable of if she could not control her rage? No one was safe around her. What if someone else got to her that way and she lashed out once again. Surely, she would not lose herself that way again- but what if she did?

CHAPTER 35
LESSONS IN LOVE

Weeks had passed since the terrible fight and Ava was not ready to go out again. She felt she needed to think things through. She was deeply disturbed by her behavior on the softball field. It was frightening that she could not remember. Scarier still was the fact that she could have taken a life. She had not been raised that way. Even though she had stopped going to church after Grant left, she still knew the difference between right and wrong. Ava was afraid of herself. She could not predict when she would black out and hurt someone if she felt threatened. The lack of self-control made her dangerous. There was something about feeling trapped or intimidated that triggered a visceral response. She would have to figure out what was happening to her. She had to learn to control her rage. Until then, no one was safe around her.

Ava began to stay around the house. She was spending more time getting to know her son once more. She was taking him for walks and learning to enjoy being his mom once again. He was such a handsome little boy, a lighter skinned version of his father. Ava had not heard from Grant in weeks and still missed him more than she cared to admit. He had been her whole world, but he had thrown her away and not looked back.

Ava and Grant Jr. were sitting inside their trailer with the front door open. The sound of a car engine got their attention and they rose from the couch to check it out. Ava's heart gave a sharp stutter as she saw that it was Grant. He was walking up to them with a confident smile on his face. Grant Jr. ran towards the steps with his arms outstretched, ecstatic to see his father. Grant rushed to his son and plucked him from the top step. He embraced him and began to spin in circles, showering Grant Jr. with kisses. Ava watched from the doorway. As Grant looked into her eyes, she slowly turned and walked back inside the house. Her heart fluttered, excitement and uncertainty warring within her mind. Grant was here; but why? When had he come back to town? Why did he not tell her he was coming home?

Grant entered the house with their son on his hip. He let him slip to his feet on the floor. Grant said, "hey Ava, don't I get a hug from you too?" Ava rolled her eyes. Grant came closer and leaned down, his face close to hers. "God, he smelled so good," Ava thought to herself. Grant softly touched his lips to hers and Ava felt herself melting into him. Without the slightest hesitation, she kissed him with all the loneliness and pain she had harbored for months while he was away. As they kissed, Ava touched both sides of his face, holding him there, still not believing he was real. Tears coursed from her eyes, between their lips and the saltiness tainted their kiss. Ava pulled back and slapped Grant's face. He stared at her and pulled her back to him, kissing her hard this time. Ava threw her arms around his neck and pulled him onto her as she leaned back onto the couch. Grant Jr. broke the spell calling out for his daddy. As Grant began to turn towards their son, Ava grabbed his face and turned him back to her. "Are you home now?" she asked him as her eyes searched his. "I'm home, baby," he said to her.

Ava left to go to the store to get something special to cook for Grant's dinner. She left the two of them home to spend some time together. She knew her son had missed his father just as much as she had. She could hardly believe he was here. She would make him a nice dinner and remind him of what they had once shared. Finally, they could become a family again. When Ava returned, she cooked, and they sat down to eat their first meal as a family. Grant walked his son over to Carl and Jenney's and returned to finish greeting Ava.

They showered together and made love most of the night. She poured all the loneliness and fear she had harbored for months during his absence into every kiss. Afterwards, Ava cried softly as he held her in his arms. She could not believe he had finally come back to her. She would never let him leave her again. They were meant to be a family, the three of them. Grant Jr. deserved to have his father with him daily. She would not have it any other way. She felt so safe in his arms, so at peace. She lay there staring up into his face until she finally fell asleep.

Ava awakened with a start. Grant was not in her bed. Where had he gone? Had she simply dreamed that he had come home to her? She tore from the room, naked and ran down the hall frantically calling for Grant. He came inside the front door holding their son just as she got to the kitchen. She stood there, panting, and breathless, her fears proven wrong. Still, she stood staring at him as though he were a dream and she was too afraid to speak. She was afraid she would wake up and Grant would be gone again. As though he could read her thoughts, Grant laughed and said, "I'm right here baby. I went to get Grant Jr. while you were sleeping." Ava stared back at him silently. Grant cleared his throat and said, "you do know you're naked right?" Ava looked down. She covered herself with her hands and ran back to her room.

The next several weeks went by quickly. Grant and Ava were inseparable. She was finally able to breathe again, knowing he had not abandoned her after all. Grant began to spend a few nights at his family home to catch up with them as well. Ava was fine with him going to see them, she knew they had missed him too. She did not like that he spent nights away from her and Grant Jr. They began to argue about it. Grant began to spend more time away. One evening after making love, Grant told her he was leaving again. He said he was moving to Anniston, Alabama to stay with his brother who was going to help him study for the ASVAB. Grant had decided to join the Army. They argued viciously. Ava told him there was no way they could survive as a family if he joined the military. She had heard how easy it was for men to cheat when they went away. Ava was afraid that he would replace her with another girl again. He had done it before. Grant insisted that he had to do what was in his own best interest. He needed to secure a better future. He said that one day he would return for her. He did not know when that would be. Devastated, Ava did not put up a fight. She told him if he left her this time, they were finished. He left the same evening.

CHAPTER 36
SNAPPED

Ava refused to be sad. She told herself she would not waste another moment mourning the loss of a relationship when Grant obviously cared so little. She would make herself forget him. She was determined to get him out of her mind once and for all. Ava began drinking again. She partied harder than ever before. She began spending less and less time with her son, once again. Wrapped in her own self-pity, she did not consider that he needed his mother.

One fall evening, Ava went to the Spur of the Moment, one of her favorite nightclubs. She was a regular there now and everyone knew her face. They also got a sense of her temper, so no one bothered her there. That Saturday night her cousin Andrew got into a fight. Ava was there and came out of the club just as the fight was ending. She saw that Andrew was hurt. She went over to find out if he was ok. He said he was fine, but Ava could see that he was still incensed. Ava glimpsed the boys that he had been fighting as they were getting into their cars. They had driven across the line to cause trouble, clearly bored with their clubs in Mississippi. Ava made sure Andrew had a ride home and she went back inside the club.

Ava began dancing, putting on a show for the men in the crowd. She knew they liked what they were seeing, so she began a seductive slow roll. Ava knew that her body had finally matured after having her son. Her small frame now had curves and her legs were petite but strong. Her once tiny breasts had developed fully, and she used them seductively. She closed her eyes, searching for that abandon, that release she used to find on the dance floor. It was elusive and escaped her. She danced harder, drank even more, and tried to ignore the errant tear trailing down her face. Angrily she wiped it away, pretending she felt nothing. She tried again to reach the carelessness she sought. Again, she thought of Grant. Frustrated, Ava stomped off the dance floor and went to the ladies' room. She washed her face and went out to get another drink. As she walked from the bar a guy caught her eye. He was about 5'7" with light brown skin and a muscular build. He was gorgeous and Ava was emboldened. She walked over to him and encircled his waist with her arms. He turned to face her and smiled. "Damn lady did you want to say something to me," he joked. Ava shook her head "no." She raised her hand to touch the side of his face and traced a path over his cheekbones and down to his chest. "My name is James, what's yours," he said. Ava did not reply. Instead she traced his lips with the tip of her finger. James was entranced. He watched as she began to dance just for him. Ava moved her body in such suggestive ways, everyone stopped to stare at the show she was putting on. She moved slowly around James, with her hand making its way around his head. When she got behind him, she leaned her body close to his. James groaned and tried to grab her arm. Ava moved out of his reach. She continued her slow prance around him, careful to maintain physical contact. This time she maneuvered her backside onto him, spooning. She lifted each of his arms and encircled herself within, grinding on him all the while. She felt him stir as his manhood began to rise and Ava stepped away. Ava left him standing there and headed for the door. She did not turn around. As the door began to close, James pushed it open and caught up to her. He grabbed Ava by the wrist and pulled her close and lowered his lips to hers. Ava put her fingers over his lips and pushed gently. She asked him if he wanted to leave and find someplace more private. James took out his keys. She walked with him to his car and laughed when she saw the make. A newer model Chevy Beretta.

Ava spent the night with James at a motel and he drove her home the next day. They began seeing each other, but Ava would not let him get to know her. She would not give him her phone number, so they only saw each other if they happened to be at the same nightclub. He was forbidden from coming to her house unless he was dropping her off. She never let him come inside. James was falling for her. He asked her to let him take her out on a proper date, but Ava refused repeatedly. She told him she only wanted one thing and if he had a problem providing that, she would find someone else. It was just that simple.

Ava began to ignore him, pretending not to see him when he beckoned for her across crowded rooms. She did not want to get close. She only wanted a distraction to keep her thoughts from returning to Grant. She began to see other men, teasing them, sleeping with them, and discarding them one by one. Ava had decided if alcohol and dirty dancing would not get Grant out of her head, she would keep sleeping around until she forgot.

The next week, Ava and Elena got dressed to go to a club in Waynesboro, Mississippi. They picked up their cousin Amanda along the way. The drinks in the club were watered down but free and Ava made a beeline for the bar. Elena and Amanda went for a view nearer the dance floor. Ava took a seat at the bar and sipped her watered drink. She surveyed the place. The club was a warehouse and had plenty of space, but it was filled nearly to capacity. The DJ was good at keeping the crowd entertained, so the energy was high. A man walked up beside Ava and ordered a drink. As he took it, he promptly spilled half of it down her shirt. Ava calmly brushed at her shirt with a napkin as the man apologized. Something in his tone made her look up at him. Ava recognized him. He was one of the guys fighting with Andrew weeks ago at the Spur. Ava said "it is fine, no problem. My shirt will dry." She turned back toward the bar. The man bumped her chair violently, as if he had stumbled. Ava caught herself to avoid falling. She said "ok what is your problem? Are you drunk? Step back please," as she raised a defensive hand. The man began cursing, calling her dirty names. Ava became angry. She felt the rage try to take over her and stifled it quickly. She took a deep breath and turned to the man once more. "Look, I do not know you and you obviously do not know me. Let's keep it that way, ok? Let's be cool." She stuck out her hand for the man to shake. He did and he walked away. Moments passed and Ava was still irritated. The evening was ruined for her. Still, she had asked her sister and cousin to come out with her, so she did not want to ask them to cut their evening short. She ordered another drink. The man returned. He started insulting her again and Ava cursed him and told him to get out of her sight. He began to advance on her threateningly. A tall gentleman interceded. He stepped between the two and put his hand in the rude guy's chest. He told him to walk away. He said, "the lady said she is good, and she clearly does not want to talk- so why don't you leave her alone." Grateful, Ava thanked him and turned back to the bar once again. The guy who had interceded on her behalf pulled up a bar stool and sat next to her. They began a conversation. Ava relaxed and the evening progressed.

At midnight, the club closed due to city restrictions. Ava walked out still talking to the man who had come to her rescue. As they got closer to her car, she noticed her sister and cousin were already inside. The man asked if he could have her phone number. Ava began to walk to the car to get something to write with, but the rude guy from before blocked her path. He began dancing around so that she could not pass. Each time she tried to go around he would dance that way, deliberately keeping her trapped. Ava gave him a shove as she shouldered under to push past the man. He grabbed her by the throat and squeezed, pushing her back against the car. Ava looked at him and saw Shane Jr.'s face staring back. Her eyes widened, fear coursing through her with sudden force. Laughing, the man let Ava go with a hard shove. He slapped her hard across the face. The fear caved under blinding anger, singeing Ava's mind. Ava slapped him back. He punched her in the mouth. Ava punched him twice in rapid succession. The man who had spent the evening talking with her was still standing behind her, watching the events unfold. He stepped close and grabbed Ava's wrists, twisting both arms behind her back. The other man grabbed her and held her in place as he licked her face on each side. His tongue left a trail of saliva from her chin to her forehead. In her mind, Ava was suddenly back in the white pickup with Sandy holding her arms, imprisoning her, sacrificing her to rape. She could feel herself losing her grip on reality. He stepped back, letting go and the man holding her arms did the same. The first guy began taunting her, laughing, and backing away. Ava was long past losing control. Her mind was a haze of red as rage incinerated her insides. The guy went to the other side of the car and Amanda jumped out. She yelled at him to leave Ava alone and the guy punched her in the mouth. Ava watched quietly from the driver's side of the car. She leaned over and reached inside the open window. She heard the man coming towards her again as she hurriedly straightened. He slapped her face again, hard, but Ava was beyond the reach of pain. All her monsters had mated, and this guy was the result. Ava knew that he was just as insane as Shane Jr. had been. He would beat her and rape her until someone stopped him. Ava was not going to lie down quietly this time. She refused to be the obedient little girl. Not this time. The monster in front of her would not get the satisfaction of seeing her cower. The man kept laughing and taunting and backpedaling. All the while he kept slapping Ava's face as he sneered. Ava continued to follow. Finally, the man seemed to notice Ava's dark expression. He stopped hitting her and his taunting ceased. He backpedaled faster. Ava smiled. She knew the exact moment he was aware of the shift in power. He turned and ran, and Ava moved swiftly but calmly after him. He went between a pair of old buildings. Ava abandoned herself to the rage. With a shrill, high-pitched scream, she grabbed onto the man's throat and pushed him against the wall. In that moment she took back her virginity. She reclaimed her innocence. She avenged the theft of her childhood. All the fear, all the shame, all the trauma culminated into that moment. The next few seconds went blank. When her focus returned, Ava was walking back towards her car holding a bloody knife. As she neared, the other man asked if she was still going to give him her phone number. She laughed "seriously?" she asked. "You're clearly delusional. After the things you just did there is no way in hell! Besides, you really should be more concerned with your friend. I left him over there bleeding in the alley." The man laughed uncertainly. Ava slowly raised the bloody knife and watched his expression turn to fear. She laughed lightly as she watched him run towards the alley. Ava got into the driver's seat and felt the adrenalin rush her all at once. Her head began to pound as her heart sped. She felt heavy perspiration cover her whole body. Her body trembled uncontrollably. She waited a moment for her vision to clear and pulled the car out into traffic. They made it to the four-way-stop as a car came racing from behind them and through the intersection, hazard lights flashing. The car turned in the direction of the hospital up ahead. Elena was incredulous. She had noticed the knife in Ava's hand. She yelled "What did you do? Did you stab that man?" Ava said in a low, steady tone, "yes, I sure did." Elena went silent for an instant. Finding her voice, she said, "how could you do that to him? You could have killed him! What the hell is wrong with you Ava?" Ava gave her sister a disbelieving glance. She could not believe what she was hearing. How could she take that monster's side? Had she not seen how he violated her? Did she even care? She was livid with her sister. Ava felt as though she had just been punched once more tonight. She shook her and tried to focus on the road.

Later that night Ava sat in a tub of scalding water, soaking away her pain. Her head ached and her lip was split open from the repeated punches. She held an ice pack to her left eye, trying to control the swelling. As she soaked, she took stock of her state of mind. She was decidedly numb. Ava did not feel any remorse. She honestly could not find an ounce of concern for the man who had attacked her. She had tried to avoid an altercation with him, but he would not leave her alone. Each time she tried to get him to leave, he had continued to taunt and harass her. Ava had been afraid of losing her temper, which is why she kept telling the man to go away. As their situation escalated, Ava began to have flashbacks. Suddenly, her attacker at the club became a composite of every man who had hurt her. All she kept thinking the whole time he was beating and taunting her was "not again, motherfucker! Not again."

EPILOGUE

Truth can be stranger than fiction and Ava had certainly learned that the hard way. For years she wondered why bad things seemed to always happen to her. She had been sexually assaulted by nearly every adult that she encountered, beginning with members of her own family. Ava could not help thinking how unfair it was. She wondered if she would ever get over the guilt and the shame. She began therapy several years later to help her deal with the trauma.

Ava learned some difficult truths about herself and some of the predators who hurt her. She learned that many children who experience sexual abuse will be sexually assaulted again later in life. Many psychologists call this a revictimization. The belief is that through harboring shame and guilt over their past trauma, survivors lack the ability to properly judge the character of future predators. Ava is still unsure how that characterization fits with her early childhood experiences. She began to focus on dealing with her trauma rather than finding someone to blame. Her therapist taught her a phrase to help her learn to cope and to put her on the path to forgiveness.

"hurt people hurt people." We often learn what we see and repeat the patterns of those who have hurt us.

Ava learned that Grandpa Harry, Carl's dad was accused of sexually abusing both his daughters. Grandma Verna knew of the abuse, and that was why she moved out of their little house. She left her children to fend for themselves in the home of a sexual predator. The children were ashamed of their father's abuse and forbidden from telling anyone what they had endured. Carl grew up in the middle of this abusive environment. Children learn what they live.

Jenney was raised in a household where children were seen, not heard. She was raped by an adult male when she was just fifteen years old. Her family did not protect or coddle her, so she never learned those skills. In fact, when her rapist was about to go to trial, Jenney's family suddenly dropped the charges. Jenney later learned that her family had accepted money from the accused in an undisclosed amount. Jenney told Ava she felt the sting of her parents' betrayal at that time.

Jimmy ended up addicted to drugs and went to prison for several years. While in prison he sent Grandma Nancy an apology letter. He revealed that he had been raped between the ages of nine and thirteen by a man who was respected in their community. Jimmy had never told anyone of his abuse until his life had spiraled out of control. His descent into drug abuse was an attempt to hide from his pain as much as it shielded him from accountability. Ava felt bad about what had happened to her brother. She had spent her whole life nearly hating him. Knowing did not change the pain he caused her, but she supposed it helped her to understand him.

Ava has yet to forgive all her attackers, especially her cousin Shane. She was informed of his death which occurred many years later. Shane had continued to live a life of crime and his life was tragically taken. Shane failed to keep his end of a drug deal and the dealers came to collect. They reportedly tortured him for hours, dragging his body behind their car until he died. Ava is working on revising her own apathetic response.

Ava felt that by not speaking out about the people who took advantage of her she was protecting and empowering them. Hurt people certainly do hurt others, but silence allows them to hide from their pain while continuing to prey on the innocent. She decided she would no longer remain complicit in their criminal behavior and she would break this generational curse.

The culture of silence must be destroyed. We must hear the cries of the children, even when they are silent. Parents, educators, extended family etc. are in unique positions to hear the silent cries, discover the hidden bruises, and ferret out the secret monsters. Ava has taken the first step by pulling back the curtain and exposing depravity's lair. She now hopes to open a dialogue of honesty within her family and to empower thousands of others like her to do the same. Her intent is that by doing so she will begin a legacy of love, truth, and transparency for the generations that are still to come.

What happens in the family, stays in the family, after all.
THE END

ABOUT THE AUTHOR

A M Young is a poet and writer whose works cover topics like social justice, women's empowerment, and romance.

She supports and champions the rights of Veterans, the LGBTQ community, and survivors of sexual assault.

Young works out of her home in Atlanta, GA. She enjoys gardening, reading, vacationing, and spoiling her grandchildren.

www.ingramcontent.com/pod-product-compliance
Lightning Source LLC
Chambersburg PA
CBHW051402290426
44108CB00015B/2118